ELISABETH RUSSELL TAYLOR

Elisabeth Russell Taylor is the author of
non-fiction books for adults and fiction for
children. She works as a freelance journalist
and French translator, and her articles have
been published in leading newspapers and
magazines. She has appeared on television
and radio on both sides of the Atlantic, and
for two years contributed regularly to the
BBC's *Woman's Hour*. The time she spent
living and working abroad and her lifelong
interest in food and its preparation proved
immensely valuable when a member of her
family was diagnosed a diabetic.

*Illustrated on the front cover is Menu 1 from
the section on Everyday Menus (see pages 72-3)*

THE DIABETIC COOKBOOK

ELISABETH RUSSELL TAYLOR

Hamlyn Paperbacks

THE DIABETIC COOKBOOK
ISBN 0 600 20280 1

First published in Great Britain 1981
by Hamlyn Paperbacks
Copyright © 1981 by Elisabeth Russell Taylor

Hamlyn Paperbacks are published by
The Hamlyn Publishing Group Ltd,
Astronaut House,
Feltham,
Middlesex, England
(Paperback Division: Hamlyn Paperbacks,
Banda House, Cambridge Grove,
Hammersmith, London W6 0LE)

*I would like to thank Barbara Argles, Judy Dinwiddie and
Jill Metcalfe for all their help with this book*

Printed and bound in Great Britain
by Cox & Wyman Ltd, Reading

CONTENTS

PREFACE

This book is the result of personal experience. I have been interested in food and its preparation throughout my adult life and, having travelled widely, made a collection of recipes from European countries, the Middle East and the United States. Five years ago, the man with whom I share my life developed diabetes. Overnight our eating habits were in peril of having to change fundamentally. As I looked into books on diabetic diet I thought the changes were going to be for the worse; I thought our diet would be bound to be both uninteresting and restricted, and I would be forced to alter cookery practices built up during 25 years at the cooker.

As it transpired, however, our diet became more rather than less interesting. My collection of recipes and previous experiments in the kitchen served me well. I had made the mistake of consulting books more concerned with diet than with gastronomy, and had failed to find one that paid equal attention to both.

I quickly discovered that what the diabetic needs is a thoroughly committed cook. A cook who knows food values; who is more than 100 per cent responsible, and never adds to or subtracts from the carbohydrate content of dishes – or slips in a teaspoonful of sugar; one whose taste buds are sensitive, who enjoys experimenting and is not a slave to habit.

The diet that I have put together has proved altogether successful in the treatment of the diabetic in my culinary care. His excellent health and enthusiasm for my cooking encouraged me to offer our ideas to other diabetics and their families.

ELISABETH RUSSELL TAYLOR

INTRODUCTION

What is diabetes?

Diabetes is a disorder that leads to an excess of sugar in the bloodstream because the pancreas fails to produce enough active insulin, a hormone, to convert the sugar efficiently into energy. The classic symptoms that lead patients to consult a doctor in the first place include great thirst, excessive urination, weight loss despite a good appetite, fatigue, itching and infections of the skin and genitals, blurred or misty vision, menstrual disorders and impotence. The aim of treatment is to restore the metabolic balance, maintain blood sugar levels to as near normal as possible, and alleviate the symptoms.

Diabetes is increasing all over the world – particularly in the more affluent countries. There are at least 600,000 known diabetics in Britain (1 – 2 per cent of the population). The controlled diabetic can live a normal working life, bear children, play games and enjoy life to the full. But there is no cure for diabetes. Once the chronic disorder is diagnosed, treatment commenced, and the diet planned, the sufferer will have to visit a physician regularly even if 'stabilised'. A diabetic whose initial treatment is confined to a diet may later have to take oral medication and eventually inject with insulin.

How is diabetes controlled?

This varies worldwide, but rough estimates suggest that about 25% of sufferers are treated by diet alone; over 25% by diet plus insulin; and about 50% by diet plus sulphonylureas tablets, which reactivate the latent capacity of cells in the pancreas to secrete insulin, or diet plus orbiguanides tablets, that cause sugar to enter the liver and muscles and so reduce the excess in the blood. Whether the physician prescribes oral medication or insulin (and in some cases the condition and treatment may change over time), it will certainly be pointed out that this is only half the treatment: diet and physical exercise also need to be regulated and regularised. By a combination of these controls diabetics can now expect to live as long as non-diabetics.

Diet alone Diabetics controlled by diet alone usually follow a sugar-free, low-carbohydrate diet. They should be careful to control their calorie intake. Grossly overweight diabetics should monitor their fat intake closely and avoid dishes cooked with butter and cream.

Tablets   Diabetics whose condition is controlled by tablets must eat the total carbohydrate and energy intake prescribed by their physician. It is best to spread the total amount equally through the day. Tablets cannot compensate for dietary excesses, and in such cases the blood sugar levels will go out of control.

Insulin   Diabetics controlled by insulin are normally allowed slightly more carbohydrate than those on tablets – and certainly more than those on diet alone – although their allowance is chosen to suit their individual needs and the type of insulin prescribed. However, they too must stick rigidly to the amount and distribution pattern of carbohydrate allotted to them. Too much carbohydrate and their systems will be overloaded with sugar; too little and they will feel limp and tired. But unlike those diabetics on tablets, those on insulin may suffer an insulin reaction. And too frequent rises in blood sugar levels are thought to be connected with the development of long-term complications.

Exercise

Exercise is essential in maintaining good general health, particularly desirable for diabetics who, when they fall ill even with a headcold, are liable to incur complications in their condition. In order to keep the blood circulating freely, and avoid thrombosis or clotting in the arteries, diabetics are advised to walk rather than take the bus or car wherever this is practicable. About 40 minutes' walk a day would be adequate for most people. Many diabetics, especially young people, may prefer to take exercise through sports or other physically active pastimes. The dietitian or physician will provide individual diabetics with advice and guidance to suit their particular needs and interests.

Insulin reactions

Insulin reactions or hypoglycaemic reactions are often referred to as 'hypos'. They occur when the sugar in the blood falls to too low a level. The diabetic experiences first a feeling of strangeness, that something is awry. She or he usually sweats, has difficulty seeing and may shake. His or her lips sometimes tingle and she or he becomes uncommonly hungry. The majority of diabetics can recognise the symptoms early, in time to take pre-emptive action. Diabetics should always carry a supply of concentrated carbohydrate, and in the event of a hypo should normally take at least three tablets of glucose or dextrasol or two lumps of sugar immediately. Ignoring the early warning signs can lead to something much more serious, such as loss of consciousness.

It is very important that diabetics school themselves to understand how they are likely to behave when they have low blood sugar, and inform their business associates, colleagues and friends so that they can take prompt action to avoid a hypo. The diabetic may become argumentative, even belligerent at these times, and may refuse to take the glucose or sugar that will set right the condition. Friends, family and associates must stand firm and take action, even if it means doing so apparently against the diabetic's will.

If a diabetic does fall unconscious without having taken glucose, syrup may be smeared on the inside of the mouth. This will lead to salivation and swallowing. A special injection, glucagon, may be necessary to restore consciousness, but this should only be attempted by someone trained to administer it. As soon as the diabetic comes round she or he should be given a warm drink sweetened with sugar and something with carbohydrate to eat: a couple of sweet biscuits may be all she or he feels like taking. If, however, he or she remains comatose, an ambulance must be called without delay. The longer the coma persists, the greater the danger of brain damage. It is strongly recommended that all diabetics carry some form of identification with them at all times, such as a special medical card or medallion, that will enable people to understand and deal with their reactions if necessary.

Diabetic coma

This is a much more serious condition than the hypo, and is its exact opposite. It is caused by an excess of sugar in the blood and an accumulation of acetone. It comes about gradually, and is preceded by symptoms of uncontrolled diabetes: loss of energy and weight with increasing thirst and constant urination. There may also be vomiting.

Illness

It is particularly important for diabetics to maintain good general health and avoid contact with infectious diseases where practicable. If they do become ill all diabetics must continue to take their usual quantity and type of medication unless this is altered by direct medical instruction. If the normal diet cannot be followed due to nausea, vomiting or simply lack of appetite, the usual amount of carbohydrate can be taken in fruit drinks or tea, coffee or other hot drinks to which sugar has been added. Regular testing for an excess of ketones (chemicals that are part of the fat-to-energy breakdown cycle in the body) in the blood and for hyperglycaemia (excess blood sugar) should be considered.

Smoking

Diabetics are advised to give up smoking – not cut down but give up! The reason is that cigarette smoking has been proved, to the satisfaction of most doctors, to lead to coronary thrombosis. Since this is a condition to which diabetics are more prone than non-sufferers, it is common sense not to aid and abet it.

Alcohol

All alcoholic drinks have a high calorie value. Diabetics on weight-reducing diets should not take any alcohol. The controlled diabetic, however, can safely take certain drinks in moderate quantities. There is no specific harm in alcohol where the weight is maintained at a reasonable level and the urine is sugar-free.

Diabetics on insulin and liable to reactions should bear in mind that alcohol has one serious disadvantage: it goes badly with low blood sugar. Since both dull the senses, it may impair judgement. A severe insulin reaction can be mistaken for drunkenness, particularly if the breath smells of alcohol. This can sometimes lead to misunderstandings with the police or strangers.

Diabetics on tablets (especially chlorpropamide) may experience flushing of the face when they drink alcohol. This may be socially disagreeable but is not dangerous.

Dry sherry; gin; brandy; white rum; whisky; vodka; dry red, white and rosé wine and champagne are free of carbohydrate. Liqueurs should be avoided. An appropriate flavouring essence may be substituted for the small quantities used for flavouring, particularly in the case of diabetics who are weight-watching conscientiously.

Note The majority of the recipes in this book are completely sugar free. Those which contain certain convenience foods as ingredients may contain a trace of sugar, but this has been taken into account in the calculation of the carbohydrate value of these recipes.

HOW TO USE THIS BOOK

One exchange equals 10 grams of carbohydrate. Likely allowances of exchanges per day range from 8 to 30 or more. Each three-course menu in this book totals either *4 or 5 exchanges per serving* – a practical number for the main meal of the day in most cases. However, since the exchange values are clearly shown for each recipe whether part of a menu or not, any diabetic should be able to fit this book into her or his own prescribed diet. The aim is to allow as much individual flexibility as possible.

For example, if a *4-exchange* menu does not provide enough carbohydrate, try adding the *1 additional exchange* which has been suggested as an option at the end of some recipes. Conversely, if *5 exchanges* are too many, choose a *4-exchange* menu or reduce the overall amount of carbohydrate by altering an accompaniment to a recipe, either by substituting another recipe from the first section or by reducing the size of the portion.

An alphabetical list of foods is also included at the end of the book showing how large a quantity of each is required to equal *1 exchange*, which should make it easier to mix and match. Obviously if someone prefers, for instance, Melba toast to brown bread or vice versa, attention to the exchange values involved means diabetics can choose for themselves. The intention is not to prescribe or restrict, but to cater for the widest possible range of tastes while also taking some of the work out of constantly planning one's own diet.

By the same token I have grouped the menus into two categories: everyday and entertaining. They are all delicious, but the cost of the food, style of presentation and richness of the ingredients varies between the sections. No-one need stick to my definitions, but by grouping the menus in this way I hope also to make choosing and planning appropriate meals easier.

I have followed the *exchange method* of calculating carbohydrate because I have found from experience that it is the most practical. Where possible I have concentrated the carbohydrate value in potatoes, rice, pasta and bread. By localising the carbohydrates, all the family can share in the same meals without any member feeling she or he alone is being confined to a diet. The diabetic member of the family will only need to count his or her intake of bread, potatoes and other carbohydrate bulk food. Diabetics adjust themselves to eating less carbohydrate than non-sufferers, and it becomes no hardship to them to confine themselves to 50g/2oz rice to accompany a main dish for which non-sufferers may require 75-100g/3-4oz to satisfy their appetites.

All foods are divided into three classes: carbohydrate, protein and fat. Protein may be eaten by diabetics in normal amounts; fat intake should be moderate (and reduced if excess weight is a problem); carbohydrate is rigidly controlled to match the individual's needs, since the hormone insulin – needed to break down carbohydrate – is missing from the diabetic's system. Carbohydrate is found in two forms – starchy and sugary – in foods such as bread, pasta, flour, rice, sugar itself, most fruit and some root vegetables. It is absent from meat, fish, salads and green vegetables, all of which may be eaten freely.

Different forms of carbohydrate are usually interchangeable in terms of exchange value, although the quality of nutrient content and the effect on blood sugars may not be. For recipes and menus bread can be substituted for potatoes, rice for pasta, and so on, according to individual or family preference.

There is no consensus view about what proportion of fat, carbohydrate and protein makes up the ideal balance for diabetics. Sufferers must rely on the advice of their dietitians. The most contentious matter is fat. Some doctors believe that animal fat may be the precursor of substances which cause arteriosclerosis, and it is generally accepted that there is an association between the level of cholesterol in the blood and a tendency to coronary thrombosis. Since cholesterol may be derived from certain types of animal fats, there has been a tendency in recent years to move away from them towards polyunsaturated fats. But although the case for polyunsaturated fats has been put forward strongly, not all of the most distinguished experts on diabetes agree.

Diabetics who prefer to try cutting down on their cholesterol intake are advised to start by replacing animal fats (butter, hard saturated margarines, suet and lard) with one of the two other types of fat: monosaturated olive or peanut oil, or polyunsaturated sunflower, cottonseed, soybean, sesame, corn or safflower oil. Foods with the highest levels of cholesterol, which should be avoided if cutting down is the aim, include egg yolk, Cheddar and other hard cheeses (not cottage cheese), meat (particularly liver, kidney and sweetbreads), milk, cream and shellfish. Cholesterol intake can also be reduced by trimming off as much visible fat as possible from meat before and after cooking.

Fibre

It cannot be stressed too firmly how important it is for diabetics to eat wholemeal bread whenever possible. Bread is easily made at home, but if bought in a shop it should be one of the following varieties: whole-wheat bloomer, wholemeal tin, rye bread or granary loaves. Wholemeal bread, made from the whole grain of the wheat, contains more of the B and E vitamins, together with essential trace minerals – copper, manganese, zinc and magnesium – and fatty acids.

In recent times the value of fibre in the diet has become better recognised. Civilisations that rely on high-fibre diets not only seem to avoid diabetes but also cancer of the colon and other diseases of the large intestine. Those peoples who do not eat refined flour or sugar do not seem prone to these diseases.

Fibre is the material in vegetables, grains, nuts and fruits that passes through the digestive system without being absorbed by it. It has been observed that fibre slows down the absorption of the carbohydrate that floods the system after a meal. It is very important for a diabetic to try and avoid dramatic changes in blood sugar levels, and for this reason fibre is thought to be particularly helpful in the diabetic's diet. However, those foods that contain the highest fibre levels also contain high amounts of carbohydrate. Perhaps the most sensible approach is to choose the major portion of one's carbohydrate allowance from fibre-rich foods.

Fibre is present in green vegetables (cabbage, spinach, salad, beans, peas, bean sprouts, broccoli) and root vegetables (particularly parsnips). It is present in fruit (particularly berries, apples with their skins, pears with their skins and citrus fruit), in pulses and legumes (lentils, white beans, red beans, chick peas and black-eyed beans) and brown rice. It may also be incorporated into the diet by the consumption of bran (some American doctors and nutrition experts currently advise an intake of 24 grams – about 1 oz – a day).

Sweeteners

Since I do not like the metallic aftertaste of artificial sweeteners, I only use them very occasionally with fruits that mask this taste, and in custards. I abstain from Sorbital altogether because it tends to have a laxative effect. Sorbital can be used in the preparation of biscuits and cakes, but I have tasted cakes and biscuits made with this product and personally found them unpalatable. I believe it is sensible to cut out what is a poor substitute for the real article, rather than go to the trouble of preparing something that cannot be served to the whole family with certainty that they will enjoy it (non-diabetics in the family will usually be more sensitive to artificial sweeteners than the diabetic). Part of the thinking behind this book is that the diabetic member of the family should be able to sit down at the table to eat the same food as other members of the family. It is important for the diabetic's psychological well-being that she or he is not encouraged to feel 'ill' – diabetes is not a disease, it is a disorder.

Bearing these points in mind it is not, I think, a great sacrifice for the family of diabetics to endeavour to acquire a savoury tooth to replace the more usual English sweet tooth. By avoiding artificial sweeteners where possible, by serving sandwiches rather than cakes at tea time, by avoiding soft drinks and omitting sugar from tea and coffee, half the battle is won.

The store cupboard

The ingredients of their store cupboards are as peculiar to individual families as the books on their shelves. Choice is determined not only by taste but also by the space available and the budget. But to make it possible to use this book to maximum efficiency, I have worked out a short list of stores that could always be kept in stock. The function of the store cupboard is, to my mind, to enable the cook to produce meals at short notice without having to make a special journey to the shops – but not simply by using pre-packed foods. It should also allow the cook to make an impulse buy of a single item in the confident knowledge that the store cupboard can provide the necessary accompaniments to make it into a meal.

Dry goods Flours for bread, sauces and seasoned flour; pulses; rice; noodles; spaghetti; oatmeal; bouillon cubes; selection of nuts and dried fruits (including prunes and apricots); tea; coffee beans and instant coffee; breakfast cereals; gelatine; artificial sweeteners; diabetic chocolate; ground almonds.
Herbs, spices and flavourings A personal selection to include curry powder; Worcestershire sauce; Dijon mustard; soy sauce; vanilla (and other essences to replace liqueurs where they are forbidden); vinegars; dried herbs; dried spices.
Cans and bottles Olive oil; tomatoes; tomato purée; anchovies; pâté de foie (and other pâté to taste); salmon; sardines; asparagus; celery hearts; consommé; rennet.
Fresh vegetables Onions; potatoes; carrots; leeks; celery; garlic; fresh ginger. According to taste, any other vegetables used consistently in salads and soups.
Fresh fruit Apples; oranges; grapefruit; bananas; lemons.
Drinks Beer; dry sherry; slimline mixers; selection of miniature liqueurs; canned unsweetened grapefruit, orange and tomato juice.
In the refrigerator Butter; margarine; cream (soured and sweet); beef dripping; lard; cheeses (if you do not have a larder); milk; yogurt; eggs; bacon; salad ingredients.
In the freezer Puff pastry; meat; ice cream; raspberries.

USEFUL FACTS AND FIGURES

Notes on metrication

In this book quantities are given in metric and Imperial measures. Exact conversion from Imperial to metric measures does not usually give very convenient working quantities and so the metric measures have been rounded off into units of 25 grams. This table below shows the recommended equivalents.

Ounces	Approx g to nearest whole figure	Recommended conversion to nearest unit of 25
1	28	25
2	57	50
3	85	75
4	113	100
5	142	150
6	170	175
7	198	200
8	227	225
9	255	250
10	283	275
11	312	300
12	340	350
13	368	375
14	396	400
15	425	425
16 (1 lb)	454	450
17	482	475
18	510	500
19	539	550
20 (1¼ lb)	567	575

Note When converting quantities over 20oz first add the appropriate figures in the centre column, then adjust to the nearest unit of 25. As a general guide, 1kg (1000g) equals 2.2lb or about 2lb 3oz. This method of conversion gives good results in nearly all cases, although in certain delicately balanced, carbohydrate-counted recipes a more accurate conversion is necessary.

Liquid measures The millilitre has been used in this book and the following table gives a few examples.

Imperial	Approx ml to nearest whole figure	Recommended ml
¼ pint	142	150 ml
½ pint	283	300 ml
¾ pint	425	450 ml
1 pint	567	600 ml
1½ pints	851	900 ml
1¾ pints	992	1000 ml (1 litre)

Spoon measures All spoon measures given in this book are level unless otherwise stated.

Can sizes At present, cans are marked with the exact (usually to the nearest whole number) metric equivalent of the Imperial weight of the contents, so we have followed this practice when giving can sizes.

Oven temperatures

The table below gives recommended equivalents.

	°C	°F	Gas Mark
Very cool	110	225	¼
	120	250	½
Cool	140	275	1
	150	300	2
Moderate	160	325	3
	180	350	4
Moderately hot	190	375	5
	200	400	6
Hot	220	425	7
	230	450	8
Very hot	240	475	9

Notes for American and Australian users

In America the 8-oz measuring cup is used. In Australia metric measures are now used in conjunction with the standard 250-ml measuring cup. The Imperial pint, used in Britain and Australia, is 20 fl oz, while the American pint is 16 fl oz. It is important to remember that the Australian tablespoon differs from both the British and American tablespoons; the table below gives a comparison. The British standard tablespoon, which has been used through this book, holds 17.7 ml, the American 14.2 ml, and the Australian 20 ml. A teaspoon holds approximately 5 ml in all three countries.

British	American	Australian
1 teaspoon	1 teaspoon	1 teaspoon
1 tablespoon	1 tablespoon	1 tablespoon
2 tablespoons	3 tablespoons	2 tablespoons
3½ tablespoons	4 tablespoons	3 tablespoons
4 tablespoons	5 tablespoons	3½ tablespoons

An Imperial/American guide to solid and liquid measures

Solid measures

IMPERIAL	AMERICAN
8 oz butter or margarine	1 cup
8 oz flour	2 cups
8 oz granulated or castor sugar	1 cup
8 oz icing sugar	1½ cups
8 oz rice	1 cup

Liquid measures

IMPERIAL	AMERICAN
¼ pint liquid	⅔ cup liquid
½ pint	1¼ cups
¾ pint	2 cups
1 pint	2½ cups
1½ pints	3¾ cups
2 pints	5 cups (2½ pints)

Note When making any of the recipes in this book, only follow one set of measures as they are not interchangeable.

RECIPES

BREAKFAST

In an effort to discover new ideas for the breakfast table, I wrote to the embassies of 106 foreign countries and asked what their nationals ate for the first meal of the day. The answers were disappointing: it seems that folk all over the world – as far-flung as Africa and Korea, South America and India – start the day on starch. The bulk of most breakfasts comes from some sort of flour made from maize, wheat or corn, or rice. Only in the wealthy countries of Northern Europe are fish, meat and cheese eaten at day-break.

I have, however, managed to extract a few ideas that seemed suitable for diabetics. Bearing in mind how important variety is in any 'diet' which is the least restrictive, I have included some unfamiliar ideas. But above all, I feel breakfasts need to be easy to prepare, nourishing but not heavy, and different from both lunch and dinner.

The Great British Breakfast is legendary. Continentals are as fulsome in their praise of our start to the day as they are damning in their assessment of the dinners with which we end it. But today only Stately Homes and British Rail maintain something of the Edwardian flavour of this meal. In the case of the former, sideboards still groan under whole hams, devilled kidneys, game pies, potted meats, potted fish, kedgeree and bowls of fresh fruit; in the case of the latter grilled bacon, eggs in different guises, porridge and kippers are offered. Although diabetics need a substantial breakfast – they are likely to have a reasonable number of exchanges to dispose of – heavy breakfasts are a mistake. In any case, pies topped with pastry, porridge and fruit *would* amount to more than their likely entitlement.

The diabetic who wishes to start with the traditional cooked breakfast can begin with a breakfast cereal (All Bran, Shredded Wheat and Weetabix are among the most highly recommended for being low in value and high in fibre); proceed to kippers or bacon and egg and tomato; and still have exchange value left over for a slice of toast and some home-made jam or marmalade and tea or coffee.

The diabetic who prefers an uncooked breakfast might start with a bowl of muesli (home-assembled) and proceed to some York ham served with Melba toast and tea or coffee. As an alternative try a plate of finely sliced hard cheese garnished with a hard-boiled egg; tomato quarters seasoned with sea-salt and black pepper; and followed by a croissant and butter, home-made jam, and tea or coffee. An all-fruit breakfast once a week also makes a pleasant and wholesome change – try unsweetened fruit juice together with fresh fruit, a handful of Brazil nuts and a few sultanas.

Melba Toast

20-g/¾-oz slice of bread equals 1 exchange

This can be made in several ways. In all cases, the bread must be completely dry and crisp. It may be made in advance and stored in an airtight container.
1.   Remove the crusts from thin slices of stale brown or white bread. Place on baking sheets and bake in a cool oven (150°C, 300°F, Gas Mark 2) for 1 hour or until crisp.
2.   Cut through sliced white bread and toast the slices on both sides.
3.   Toast pieces of sliced bread on both sides. While still warm, split the toast with a sharp knife and toast the resulting two pieces on the untoasted sides.

Exchange-free Jam

Negligible when used in small amounts during the week

Cooking time about 30 minutes

225g/8oz strawberries, hulled
4 artificial sweetener tablets
1 teaspoon powdered gelatine

1 tablespoon water
1 teaspoon lemon juice

Quarter the strawberries and place in a heavy pan over a very low heat until the juice runs. Boil quickly for 5 minutes. Add the artificial sweetener. Dissolve the gelatine in the water and lemon juice over a low heat and add to the fruit. Turn into a bowl and, when cold, refrigerate. This jam will not keep for more than 1 week and must be stored in the refrigerator.

Note   This jam may be made equally well with raspberries, apricots, peaches, blackberries and other fruits. If made with apples, it turns into apple sauce but flavoured with ginger makes an interesting change. Try adding chopped blanched almonds to apricot or peach jam.

Exchange-free Marmalade

Negligible when used in small amounts during the week

Cooking time about 45 minutes

2 oranges (150-175g/5-6oz gross weight)
600ml/1 pint water

1 teaspoon powdered gelatine
juice of ½ lemon
4-8 artificial sweetener tablets

Boil the oranges whole in the water until cooked – about 30 minutes in a pressure cooker. Drain. Reserve 4 tablespoons of the cooking water. Chop the oranges and discard the pips. Place in a bowl. Dissolve the gelatine in the cooking water and lemon juice with the artificial sweetener added. Pour over the oranges. When cold, store in the refrigerator. This marmalade will not keep for more than 1 week and so it is best made in small quantities. Use on toast, scones and ice-cream.

Kedgeree

10 exchanges per recipe
Serves 4

Cooking time about 35 minutes

450g/1lb smoked haddock
1 onion, chopped
75g/3oz butter
100g/4oz long-grain rice
½ teaspoon curry powder or paste

To garnish
2 hard-boiled eggs, quartered
1 tablespoon chopped fresh parsley

Simmer the haddock in water for about 10 minutes. Drain and flake the fish, discarding the skin and bones. Reserve the cooking liquid. Brown the onion in 25g/1oz butter and stir in the rice. When the rice has absorbed the butter, add the curry powder or paste. Make up the fish cooking liquid to 450ml/¾ pint and pour on to the rice. When the rice is cooked, mix in the fish and remaining butter. Garnish with the hard-boiled eggs and parsley.

Oatmeal Fries

8 exchanges per recipe
Serves 4

Cooking time 10 minutes

4 tablespoons dry oatmeal
50g/2oz plain flour
1 tablespoon baking powder
4 tablespoons grated cheese
½ teaspoon dry mustard

salt and pepper
175ml/6fl oz milk
175ml/6fl oz water
oil for shallow frying

Liquidise the ingredients in a blender to a batter. Heat the oil and fry the oatmeal mixture in spoonfuls until golden brown and crisp, about 10 minutes. Drain on kitchen paper and serve with bacon and eggs.

Mexican Scrambled Eggs

Serves 2

Cooking time 10 minutes

2 small tomatoes
1 small onion
1-2 green chillies

25g/1oz butter
4 eggs, lightly beaten
salt and pepper

Chop the tomatoes, onion and chillies finely. Melt the butter in a pan and add the vegetables. Stir the mixture and cook for 5 minutes. Add the eggs and continue stirring until the eggs are set. Season well. Serve at once with French bread (*20g/¾oz bread equals 1 exchange*).

Gouda Pie

4 exchanges per recipe
Serves 4

Cooking time 20-30 minutes
Oven temperature Hot 220°C,
425°F, Gas Mark 7

100g/4oz frozen flaky pastry
225g/8oz Gouda cheese
4-6 mushrooms, sliced

2-3 tomatoes
25g/1oz butter, melted
salt and pepper

Roll out the pastry thinly and use to line a Swiss roll tin measuring approximately 28 x 20cm/11 x 8inches. Prick the base with a fork. Cover with slices of Gouda cheese, arrange a diagonal line of mushrooms and cover the remainder of the cheese with thinly sliced tomatoes. Brush the mushrooms with the butter and season generously. Bake in a hot oven for 20-30 minutes.

Swiss Bircher Muesli

This is the quantity suggested by Dr. Bircher-Benner and I am quoting it precisely because he considered it a perfectly balanced meal.

3 exchanges per recipe
Serves 1

1 tablespoon oatmeal
3 tablespoons water
1 large apple (or the same quantity of a preferred fruit)

juice of ½ lemon
2 tablespoons single cream
1 tablespoon chopped nuts

Soak the oatmeal overnight in the water. In the morning, peel and grate the apple, then mix at once with the lemon juice to prevent discolouring. Blend with the soaked oatmeal and cream. Sprinkle over the chopped nuts and serve at once. Use presoaked prunes or seedless raisins when fresh fruit is not available.

Note   The only thing I would add is that it is a mistake to peel the apple since only the dustbin would then benefit from the goodness in and just beneath the peel.

A French Breakfast

Croissant, brioche and café au lait are perfectly suitable for an English diabetic's breakfast. A medium sized croissant and brioche are counted as having *2 exchanges* although this is a slightly difficult measurement to judge because different brioche and croissant contain different amounts of flour and butter — and, of course, the 'lait' must be counted, too. So, if you want 2 croissant, the coffee must be taken black in a *4-exchange* breakfast.

Canadian Potato Pancakes

12 exchanges per recipe
Serves 4

Cooking time 15 minutes

1 onion, finely chopped
100g/4oz bacon, diced
4 50g/2oz potatoes, grated

1 egg
100g/4oz flour
salt and pepper

Fry the onion and bacon together. Add the remaining ingredients and mix well. Drop tablespoons of the mixture on to a well-greased frying pan and brown on both sides.

Nigerian Banana and Coconut Pudding

4½ exchanges per recipe
Serves 4

Cooking time 20-30 minutes
Oven temperature Hot 230°C,
450°F, Gas Mark 8

1 275-g/10-oz coconut
300ml/½ pint coconut milk
(see method)
2 eggs

1 teaspoon powdered artificial
sweetener
2 bananas

Break the coconut and reserve the milk – if there is not quite 300ml/½ pint add cow's milk to make up the quantity. Grate the coconut, beat the eggs with the sweetener and add the coconut milk. Peel and mash the bananas and blend into the mixture. Butter a pie dish and pour in the mixture. Bake in a hot oven for 20-30 minutes.

An Israeli Breakfast

The Israeli starts the day with a hearty salad consisting of ripe juicy tomatoes (of a type we cannot obtain), cucumbers, green peppers, radishes and spring onions all finely chopped and seasoned with lemon juice and olive oil. This is accompanied by green olives, smoked or pickled fish and a variety of cheeses. The fish include smoked white fish, smoked tuna and various types of herring. All sorts of cheeses, including goat's cheese, is served and so too are yogurt, soured cream and leben, a low-fat soured milk product (which is obtainable in London from the Lebanese food centre). They normally have an egg with this and fresh rolls and butter. They drink lemon tea. This would be a very good, well balanced, low carbohydrate meal for a diabetic.

Morning Coffee

Morning coffee, taken consistently at the time prescribed, normally has an *exchange* allowance which can take care of a buttered bun, a toasted teacake, a couple of scones. Or the diabetic may have to make do with two semi-sweet biscuits and a cup of tea. This break has to be taken on the dot by those diabetics on insulin who spend every morning doing the same job and using up the same amount of energy; the morning injection having coped with the breakfast carbohydrate, is poised around coffee time for another lot to deal with. If it fails to get it, the result is a reaction.

Afternoon Tea

Afternoon tea is slightly more flexible than morning coffee. The fast acting insulin has by now been consumed by the system which is left coasting on the longer acting insulin. The diet may permit very few *exchanges* and the diabetic may have to content himself with a cup of tea and a couple of semi-sweet biscuits or a piece of fresh fruit. However, where the *exchange* allowance is more generous, scones are a useful addition, so too is Melba toast. An open sandwich with its carbohydrate rigidly confined to the base, can provide a solution for a hungry person.

Late Night Extra

It is usual for diabetics to take a hot drink and a couple of semi-sweet biscuits before retiring. Those diabetics on insulin will need some carbohydrate to cope with the insulin gently let into the system during sleep.

All diabetics should have glucose tablets, water, biscuits and sweetened drinks on the bedside table. Any insulin reaction during the night is likely to wake the sufferer, who should have everything ready to cope with it without getting up.

LUNCH

Diabetics who work away from home have various alternatives to consider at lunch time: (1) a packed lunch prepared at home; (2) bought sandwiches and fruit; (3) pub and restaurant lunches.

It may be desirable for social reasons to eat out at mid-day, and this is quite feasible if the diabetic eats 'à la carte'. Any set menu tends to include unsuitable pudding courses, and the soup may be thickened with flour so that counting exchanges can be hazardous. Enquiries about the composition of dishes may be met by an unfriendly response – or lied about.

A packed lunch has a number of advantages: it tastes as good as the cook can make it; it is economical; it does not have to be queued for and it can contain the precise number of exchanges required. It need not be boring or second-best to a restaurant meal. The diabetic's internal lunch clock strikes the same hour as everyone else's. A delay in eating may lead to a hypo.

Today we have containers that can keep food hot or cold. There are vacuum flasks, insulated jars and 'seal-fresh' polythene containers for use in temperate weather; for use in extreme heat or cold there are insulated box-shaped picnic bags which keep food hot for approximately 4 hours and chilled for 8 hours. Firms that make these containers make sachets which can be frozen in the freezer overnight and placed in the picnic box in the morning to ensure really cold food at lunch time – even in a heat-wave.

A few points to watch out for: plan to keep the salad container for salad and do not include onion in the mixture. Keep a separate container for fish dishes and another for meat dishes. To avoid mixing them up (if you do not have a particularly highly developed sense of smell), mark the containers with nail-varnish. The polythene used for containers has a tendency to retain something of the smell of the food packed in it. Wrap sandwiches in greaseproof paper or foil before slipping them into a sealed polythene container. And before packing hot food into a vacuum flask, heat the flask by filling it to the brim with boiling water. Leave for 5 minutes, then pour out the water. Fill the flask *to the top* with the hot food. Get accustomed to taking courses from the menus in this book. Before packing chilled food into a vacuum flask, slide ice cubes into the flask. Put the lid on the flask and leave for 5 minutes. Pour away the ice and pour in the chilled food. Fill the flask to the top. There are 450 ml/¾ pint wide-necked flasks ideal for single portions of soup and solid food.

The ideal carrier in which to transport a packed lunch is one in which all items are guaranteed to maintain an upright position.

The ideal packed lunch might include salad with a vinaigrette dressing packed in a small bottle separately; cheeses, cold meats and a soup, possibly without exchange value, together with a can of beer and carefully weighed out oatcakes or bread rolls. This combination would provide a more interesting, satisfying meal with more goodness than is normally obtainable at the pub counter or sandwich bar.

Keep a salt mill, a pepper mill, coffee beans and tea in the office. Packed lunches do not have to be eaten out of their containers. I recommend as part of the office equipment paper napkins, glasses, cups and saucers, soup bowls, plates, cutlery, a coffee grinder, jug or percolator, tea pot. Arrange to have milk delivered daily, if possible. Keep emergency rations of concentrated carbohydrate, too, eg. confectionery, plain sweet biscuits and glucose tablets.

Lunch at home is normally less relaxed than dinner time. I think the more elaborate meal is best kept for the evening.

Snacks suitable for lunch time can be prepared from eggs – I suggest omelettes as a particularly easy, quick and interesting meal; salads, cold meats, cheeses and open sandwiches.

Omelette

Serves 2   *Cooking time about 5 minutes*

3 (size 2) large eggs   3 teaspoons cold water
salt and pepper   15g/½oz butter

Break the eggs into a bowl, add the seasoning and water. Beat very lightly. Heat a frying pan gently, add the butter and turn up the heat. When the butter is sizzling, pour in the egg mixture. Draw the cooked egg from the edge of the pan inwards so that the liquid egg runs through to cook on the pan base. While the surface is still runny, either fold over one third of the omelette away from the pan handle, shake the omelette to the edge of the pan and tip it over on to a warm serving plate, or spoon a filling in the centre, fold over and tip it out. Serve with a green salad.

Try these omelette mixture fillings: chopped fresh herbs or cheese; fried mushrooms; a combination of diced fried potato and onions; flaked fish in a thick cheese sauce.

The omelette itself is *exchange-free* so it is well worth experimenting with small quantities of vegetable, nut, meat or fish fillings to make a lunch dish.

Cheese Soufflé

3½ exchanges per recipe
Serves 4

Cooking time 40 minutes
Oven temperature Moderately Hot
200°C, 400°F, Gas Mark 6

25g/1oz butter
25g/1oz flour
300ml/½ pint milk
50g/2oz grated Parmesan cheese

(or 25g/1oz Gruyère and
25g/1oz Parmesan)
4 (size 2) large eggs, separated
salt and pepper

Melt the butter, remove from the heat and add the flour. Mix well and blend in the milk. Stir until the mixture is smooth. Return to the heat, stirring continuously, for about 10 minutes or leave to simmer very, very gently on an asbestos mat. Stir in the cheese and egg yolks. Season. (This mixture may be prepared in advance and kept cool for the addition of the stiffly beaten egg whites.) Whisk the egg whites until they form peaks. Tip half on to the basic mixture. Using a metal spoon, cut down through the mixture, across the bottom and lift some mixture up over the egg white. Mix in the remaining egg white in the same way. Turn into a buttered soufflé dish and bake in a moderately hot oven for 25 minutes.

Piperade

Serves 2

Cooking time about 18 minutes

2 onions, sliced
1 green pepper, seeded and sliced
   thinly
25g/1oz butter

2 large tomatoes, peeled and
   chopped
salt and pepper
4 eggs

Cook the onion and pepper in the butter until soft but not brown. Add the tomato and cook for 3 minutes. Season. Beat the eggs lightly with salt and pepper, pour on to the vegetables and stir over a medium heat until the eggs are just set but still creamy. Serve at once with French bread *(20 g/¾oz bread equals 1 exchange)* and a Mixed green salad (see page 49).

Spinach Soufflé

4½ *exchanges per recipe*
Serves 4

Cooking time 40–45 minutes
Oven temperature Hot 220°C,
425°F, Gas Mark 7

350g/12oz frozen chopped
   spinach, thawed
50g/2oz butter
50g/2oz flour
150ml/¼ pint milk
150ml/¼ pint single cream

salt and pepper
grated nutmeg
4 eggs, separated
4 tablespoons grated Gruyère
   cheese

Grease a 1.5-litre/2½-pint soufflé dish. Drain the spinach in a strainer. Melt the butter in a large pan, remove from the heat and add the flour, mixing well. Blend in the milk and cream. Bring to the boil, stirring all the time. Add the spinach and return to the boil. Season with salt, pepper and nutmeg. Beat in the egg yolks. Whisk the egg whites stiffly and gently fold into the mixture. Pour into the prepared soufflé dish and sprinkle with the cheese. Bake in a hot oven for 20-25 minutes or until well risen. Serve immediately.

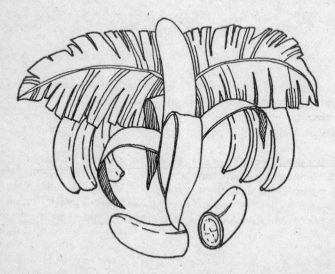

Quiche Paysanne

11 exchanges per recipe   *Cooking time about 45 minutes*
Oven temperature Hot 220°C, 425°F, Gas Mark 7, then Moderately Hot 190°C, 375°F, Gas Mark 5
Serves 4

175g/6oz wholemeal shortcrust pastry (see page 65)
40g/1½oz butter
1 medium onion, chopped
4 gammon rashers, chopped
100g/4oz mushrooms, chopped
1 100-g/4-oz cooked potato, diced

salt and pepper
2 (size 2) large eggs
150ml/¼ pint single cream
50g/2oz Cheddar cheese, grated
chopped fresh parsley to garnish

Make the pastry, roll out and use to line a 20-23 cm/8-9 inch flan tin or ring. Line with foil and bake blind in the centre of a hot oven for 15 minutes. Meanwhile, melt 15g/½oz of the butter and gently fry the onion and gammon for about 5 minutes. Add the mushrooms and continue cooking for a further 5 minutes. Add the remaining butter with the diced potato and cook again for 5 minutes. Season well. Beat the eggs with the cream and seasoning. Remove the foil from the pastry case, spread the vegetables in the case, pour over the egg mixture and top with the cheese. Bake in a moderately hot oven for 25-30 minutes or until set. Garnish with parsley. Serve hot or cold.

Bacon/Banana Rolls

2 exchanges per recipe   *Cooking time 10 minutes*
Serves 2

2 100-g/4-oz bananas
4-6 rashers streaky Canadian bacon, cut to bind round banana pieces

15g/½oz butter

Cut each banana into 4 pieces. Bind the bacon round the banana pieces and attach with wooden cocktail sticks. Fry gently in the butter until the bacon is crisp. The combination of flavours is as delicious as it is unusual. Before serving, remove the cocktail sticks. Serve with a side plate of Leaf spinach (see page 41).

Liver Pâté Crescents

7½ exchanges per recipe
Makes 8

Cooking time 25-30 minutes
Oven temperature Moderately Hot
200°C, 400°F, Gas Mark 6

1 212-g/7½-oz packet frozen puff
  pastry

175g/6oz chicken liver pâté
  (see page 124)
beaten egg to glaze

Thaw the pastry and roll out thinly into a rectangle. Cut into 4 squares
and then cut each across into a triangle. Spread with pâté and roll up
from the tip of the triangle, sealing the end with water. Twist into a
crescent shape and brush with beaten egg. Place on a baking sheet and
bake in a moderately hot oven for 25-30 minutes until golden brown.
Serve with a salad.

Stuffed Cucumber

6 exchanges per recipe
Serves 4

1-1½ cucumbers, cut into 8
  5cm/2-inch chunks
175g/6oz cream cheese
2 tablespoons milk

4 tablespoons seedless raisins,
  soaked in 2 teaspoons lemon
  juice
2 dessert apples
salt

Remove the seeds from the cucumber chunks, sprinkle with salt and
leave to stand for at least 1 hour. Rinse and dry with kitchen paper. Beat
the cream cheese with the milk and add the raisins. Chop the unpeeled
apples and mix into the cheese mixture. Spoon this mixture into the
hollow cucumber chunks. Serve at once.

Red Cabbage Salad

Serves 4   *Cooking time 10 minutes*

1 small head red cabbage
  (about 675g/1½lb)
4 tablespoons wine vinegar
6 rashers streaky bacon
1 teaspoon Dijon mustard

vinaigrette dressing (see page 59)
50g/2oz strong Cheddar,
  Gruyère or Emmenthal cheese,
  grated

Quarter the cabbage and remove the core. Shred the leaves very finely. Bring the vinegar to the boil and pour over the cabbage. Grill the bacon until very crisp, drain on kitchen paper and crumble. Add the Dijon mustard to the vinaigrette dressing. Just before serving, pour the dressing over the cabbage and scatter the bacon and cheese on top.

Lentil Rissoles

7 exchanges per recipe   *Cooking time about 1 hour*
Serves 2

75g/3oz brown or green lentils
40g/1½oz dry breadcrumbs
salt and pepper

1 egg, beaten
½ teaspoon mild curry powder
oil for frying

Cook the lentils in boiling salted water for 30-40 minutes until tender. Liquidise in a blender with a minimum of the cooking water. Add the breadcrumbs, seasoning and curry powder. Stir in the beaten egg and mix well. Cool and chill in the refrigerator for at least 3 hours. Fry in spoonfuls in very hot oil for about 10 minutes or until thoroughly brown on both sides.

Potato Pancakes

8½ exchanges per recipe
Serves 4

Cooking time 10 minutes

450g/1lb uncooked potatoes,
   grated
1 small cooked potato, mashed
1 tablespoon flour
1 egg

salt and pepper
2-3 tablespoons milk
4 tablespoons oil
25g/1oz butter

Mix the grated and mashed potatoes together. Add the flour, beaten egg, seasoning and enough milk to make a thin batter. Heat the oil in a frying pan and add the butter. When frothing, drop in the batter in spoonfuls and fry until brown round the edges on both sides.

American Hamburgers and Batter Pudding

4½ exchanges per recipe
Serves 2

Cooking time 40 minutes
Oven temperature Hot 230°C,
   425°F, Gas Mark 8

6 tablespoons milk
50g/2oz flour
1 egg
salt and pepper

25g/1oz beef dripping
2 95% meat American-style
   hamburgers

Put the milk, flour, egg and salt and pepper into a blender and liquidise thoroughly. Put the beef dripping into an ovenproof dish in the oven until it is smoking hot. Pour in the batter. Cook for 40 minutes. Grill the hamburgers as directed on the packet – or for a little less time if you like meat pink. Serve the batter pudding with the hamburgers and Mixed green salad (see page 49).

Toast Toppings

Fried egg; scrambled egg; grilled tomatoes; grilled mushrooms; sliced fried kidney; fried herring roes; fried calves' brains garnished with lemon slices; diced cooked chicken tossed in butter, drained and reheated in 1 tablespoon cream and sprinkled with cayenne pepper, or in a béchamel sauce sprinkled with Parmesan and browned under the grill;

sardines; grilled bacon; grilled mushrooms garnished with green stoned olives.

Stuffed Eggs

Cut hard-boiled eggs in two lengthways. Remove the yolks and mash with mayonnaise and one of the following: anchovy sauce, curry powder, herbs or grated cheese. Pipe or spoon back into the whites.

Cheese Wafers

10 wafers equal 1 exchange

Cooking time 6-7 minutes
Oven temperature Very Hot 240°C, 475°F, Gas Mark 9

Sandwich together unsweetened ice-cream wafers with grated Cheddar, Parmesan and enough double cream to make the mixture spreadable. Place on a baking tray and bake for 6-7 minutes.

Sandwiches

The sandwich is surely the most adaptable snack. It is easy and quick to make; it can assume the simple guise of cheese and pickle in 'plastic' bread or Scandinavian sophistication – open on pumpernikel. Fillings for sandwiches are usually available from fresh and canned goods in the store cupboard, and many can be made in advance and kept in the freezer.

Open sandwiches, for the diabetic, are probably one of the most useful snacks. A single slice of wholemeal or rye bread for the base may contain no more than *1 exchange* and a meat, fish, vegetable, cheese or egg topping may be made *without any exchange* value. A sandwich of this type is more nutritious than, say, a sweet biscuit – and more filling. It also contains more fibre.

Each recipe is enough to make 2 large open sandwiches.

Suggestions for fillings:
Corned beef, potato salad and black olives
Scrambled egg, salmon and snipped chives (smoked salmon would be nicest)

Roast beef with rémoulade sauce (see page 58)
Brisket of beef with rémoulade sauce (see page 58)
Liver pâté and cucumber relish (see page 60)
Salami and scrambled egg
Tomato with cheese mayonnaise (see page 58)
Tomato, scrambled egg and anchovy fillets
Fried cod's roe and rémoulade sauce (see page 58)
Ham, pineapple and mayonnaise (see page 57)
Hard cheese and strawberry jam (see page 21)
Banana, sultanas and walnut pieces
Grated Cheddar cheese and chutney
Chicken and ham on curry butter (see page 63)
Haddock on anchovy butter (see page 61)
Peeled shrimps in mayonnaise (see page 57) garnished with lemon
Matsje herring with onion rings
Roast or grilled chicken on lettuce garnished with crisp fried bacon

Egg Salad

2 hard-boiled eggs
2 tablespoons mayonnaise
2 spring onions, chopped, or 1
  teaspoon chopped chives

½ teaspoon French mustard
pinch celery salt

Mash the hard-boiled eggs with a fork. Mix well with the remaining ingredients.

Salmon Salad

1 212-g/7½-oz can red salmon
2 tablespoons mayonnaise
2 tablespoons chopped cucumber

1 tablespoon chopped spring
  onion
salt and black pepper

Drain and flake the salmon. Mix well with the remaining ingredients.

Ham and Chicken

50g/2oz cooked chicken
50g/2oz cooked ham
2 tablespoons mayonnaise

1 tablespoon chopped parsley
salt and pepper

Chop the chicken and ham. Mix well with the remaining ingredients.

Cream Cheese and Olive

50g/2oz cream cheese
3 stuffed green olives, chopped

1 tablespoon mayonnaise
1 tablespoon double cream

Beat the cream cheese and stir in the remaining ingredients.

VEGETABLE DISHES

Braised Celery

Serves 4   *Cooking time 1 hour*

1 head of celery
1 carrot, diced
1 onion, chopped
2 rashers of bacon, chopped

25g/1oz butter
600ml/1 pint stock (see page 61)
¼ teaspoon crushed fennel seeds

Wash the celery and trim each stick into 7.5-10-cm/3-4-inch lengths. Blanch in boiling water for 10 minutes. Drain. Sauté the carrot, onion and bacon in the butter. Place the celery on top and just cover with stock. Sprinkle with the fennel seed. Bring to the boil and simmer for about 45 minutes or until tender.

Cabbage with Caraway Seed

Serves 4   *Cooking time 8-10 minutes*

450g/1lb cabbage
salt and pepper

25g/1oz butter
½ teaspoon caraway seeds

Shred the cabbage. Cook in boiling salted water for 5-8 minutes until just tender. Drain and splash with cold water to refresh. Melt the butter, add the caraway seeds and toss the cabbage in this to reheat. Add seasoning and serve at once.

Note Experiment with other herbs such as parsley, thyme or chives instead of caraway.

Green Beans with Nuts

Serves 4   *Cooking time about 20 minutes*

450g/1lb green beans, French or   25g/1oz butter
  runner   50g/2oz salted almonds

Slice the beans or leave whole depending on type. Cook in boiling salted
water for about 15 minutes until tender. Melt the butter, sauté the nuts
and add to the drained beans.

Grilled Tomatoes

Serves 4   *Cooking time 5 minutes*

4 large tomatoes   ½ teaspoon chopped marjoram,
25g/1oz butter   oregano or basil
salt and pepper

Cut the tomatoes in half and place cut side down on the grill rack. Grill
for 2 minutes. Turn over, dot with butter and sprinkle with seasoning.
Grill until just soft. Sprinkle with chopped herbs and serve at once.

Hot Cucumber

2 exchanges per recipe   *Cooking time 30 minutes*
Serves 4   *Oven temperature Moderate*
                                   180°C, 350°F, Gas Mark 4

1 large cucumber   300ml/½ pint single cream
salt and pepper   1 teaspoon chopped fresh
25g/1oz butter   tarragon
25g/1oz plain flour

Peel the cucumber and cut into 1-cm/½-inch slices. Poach in salted
water for 15 minutes. Meanwhile, melt the butter, remove from the heat
and mix in the flour. Blend in the cream and stir until smooth. Return to
the heat and stir continuously until the mixture reaches boiling point.
Add seasoning and the tarragon. Drain the cucumber and place in an
ovenproof dish. Spoon over the sauce and heat through in a moderate
oven.

Beetroot in Soured Cream

4 exchanges per recipe   *Cooking time about 10 minutes*
Serves 4

450g/1lb cooked beetroot, diced   25g/1oz butter
   in 2.5-cm/1-inch cubes, or   salt and pepper
   whole baby beets   150ml/¼ pint soured cream

Add the beetroot to the melted butter. Season and toss over the heat
until hot. Add the soured cream and heat until the cream is hot but not
boiling.

Braised Endive or Chicory

Serves 4   *Cooking time about 1 hour*
                                    Oven temperature Cool
                                    *   150°C, 300°F, Gas Mark 2*

450g/1lb chicory   squeeze of lemon juice
50g/2oz butter   salt and pepper

Halve or quarter the chicory heads lengthwise. Blanch in boiling salted
water for 1 minute. Drain. Melt half the butter in a pan or casserole. Lay
the chicory evenly over the base. Add 150ml/¼ pint water, squeeze of
lemon juice and seasoning. Dot with the remaining butter. Cover and
simmer, or place in a cool oven for 1 hour. (If cooking in the oven, use 3
tablespoons water instead of 150ml/¼ pint.)

Cucumber in Soured Cream

Serves 4   *Cooking time about 10 minutes*

1 large cucumber   ½ teaspoon chopped fresh dill,
salt and pepper   chervil or parsley
150ml/¼ pint soured cream

Peel the cucumber, cut into four lengthwise and across in 2.5-cm/1-inch
pieces. Cook in boiling salted water for 7-10 minutes until just tender.
Drain, return to the pan and add the soured cream and seasoning. Heat
gently without boiling. Sprinkle with the chopped herbs.

Fennel in Cream Sauce

2 exchanges per recipe
Serves 4

Cooking time 25 minutes

2 heads of fennel
salt and pepper
25g/1oz butter

25g/1oz plain flour
150ml/¼ pint single cream

Wash, trim and quarter the fennel. Cook in boiling salted water for 15 minutes or until tender. Drain and reserve 150ml/¼ pint of the liquid. Melt the butter, remove from the heat and add the flour. Mix well and blend in the reserved liquid and the cream. Stir until smooth then return to the heat and stir until boiling. Simmer for 1 minute. Season to taste and pour over the fennel.

Note Celery hearts may be substituted for the fennel.

Leaf Spinach

Serves 4

Cooking time 10 minutes

1kg/2lb spinach
50g/2oz butter

salt and pepper
generous pinch grated nutmeg

Wash the spinach thoroughly. Place in a large pan without adding water and cook for about 5 minutes. Drain and chop roughly. Squeeze between 2 plates to remove excess water. Melt the butter in the pan, add the spinach and toss to reheat. Add seasoning and nutmeg.

Note Chard may be treated the same way. Remove the white centre stalks and cook these as a separate vegetable.

Braised Mushrooms

Serves 4　　　　　　　　　　*Cooking time 15 minutes*

450g/1lb button mushrooms
25g/1oz butter
1 shallot or small onion, chopped

½ teaspoon crushed coriander
　seeds
salt and pepper
squeeze of lemon juice

Wipe the mushrooms. Trim the base of the stems. Leave whole or quarter if large. Melt the butter, add the shallot, mushrooms, coriander, seasoning and lemon juice. Cover and cook gently for about 15 minutes.

Vichy Carrots

2 exchanges per recipe
Serves 4

Cooking time about 20 minutes

450g/1lb carrots
salt and pepper
sprig of mint

25g/1oz butter
chopped fresh mint or parsley
　to garnish

Leave young carrots whole or slice old carrots. Place in a pan with just enough water to cover. Add a pinch of salt, sprig of mint and the butter. Cover and bring to the boil. Remove the lid and continue cooking, allowing the water to evaporate, until the carrots are cooked and the liquid reduced to a buttery glaze. Add seasoning to taste and garnish with mint or parsley.

Braised Leeks

Serves 4　　　　　　　　　　*Cooking time about 40 minutes*

1kg/2lb leeks
50g/2oz butter
1 carrot, chopped
1 onion, chopped

1 stick of celery, chopped
600ml/1 pint stock
salt and pepper
chopped fresh parsley to garnish

Wash and trim the leeks. Cut in half lengthwise to remove any grit between the leaves. Blanch in boiling salted water for 5 minutes. Melt the butter, add the chopped vegetables and allow to brown lightly. Lay the leeks on top. Pour over the stock, add seasoning and simmer for about 20 minutes or until the leeks are cooked. Remove the leeks to a warmed serving dish. Reduce the liquid in the pan to a syrupy consistency and season to taste. Strain the liquid over the leeks and sprinkle with chopped parsley.

Fried Aubergine

2 exchanges per recipe
Serves 4

Cooking time about 10 minutes

2 medium aubergines
salt

25g/1oz seasoned flour
  (see page 64)
oil and butter for frying

Wipe, but do not peel, the aubergines. Cut into 6-mm/¼-inch slices. Sprinkle with salt and leave for 30 minutes. Rinse and pat dry with kitchen paper. Dip the slices in seasoned flour and fry carefully in oil and butter, using a little to start with and adding more as required. Drain on kitchen paper before serving.

Buttered Courgettes

Serves 4

Cooking time about 25 minutes

675g/1½lb courgettes
50g/2oz butter
salt and pepper

½ teaspoon chopped fresh
  tarragon or 1 teaspoon chopped
  fresh parsley

Cut the courgettes in 1-cm/½-inch slices. Blanch in boiling salted water for 5 minutes. Melt the butter, add the courgettes and seasoning. Cover and cook slowly for about 20 minutes until tender. Sprinkle with herbs.

Braised Onions

Serves 4   *Cooking time about 1 hour*

4 large or 8 small onions
50g/2oz butter   300ml/½ pint stock (see page 61)
1 carrot, chopped   salt and pepper
1 stick of celery, sliced   chopped fresh parsley to garnish

Brown the whole onions in the melted butter. Set aside. Brown the
carrot and celery. Replace the onions and add the stock. Bring to the boil
and simmer for about 45 minutes or until the onions are tender. Lift the
onions on to a warmed serving dish. Reduce the liquid in the pan to a
syrupy consistency. Season and strain over the onions. Sprinkle with
chopped parsley.

Note This dish is best cooked in a flameproof casserole in which the
onions have to be tightly packed.

Pourgouri

12 exchanges per recipe   *Cooking time 20 minutes*
Serves 4

25g/1oz butter   900ml/1½ pints stock
350g/12oz dry cracked wheat or   (see page 61)
  bulghur   salt and pepper

Melt the butter in a large pan and lightly brown the cracked wheat. Add
the stock, cover and simmer for about 15 minutes until the liquid is
absorbed and the grains are cooked. Add seasoning, if necessary.

Note Cracked wheat is obtainable from health food shops or Greek,
Turkish and Middle Eastern grocers. It is a very tasty substitute for rice.

Pan-Roasted Potatoes

6 exchanges per recipe
Serves 4

Cooking time 20-30 minutes

450g/1lb new potatoes
  (old potatoes will do)

olive oil

Scrape new potatoes or if using old potatoes, peel and cut in half. Place in a heavy flameproof casserole and pour over olive oil to come half-way up the potatoes. Then cover with cold water. Place the casserole over a high heat and bring to a rapid boil – the oil and water need to amalgamate. Cook briskly for between 20-30 minutes, according to the age of the potatoes. The liquid will evaporate and the potatoes will be very crisp on the outside and soft inside.

Note Although this dish is heavy on olive oil (and no other oil will produce the correct result), cooking on top of the cooker is a cheaper method than using the oven.

Duchesse Potatoes

6 exchanges per recipe
Serves 4

Cooking time 50 minutes
Oven temperature Moderately Hot
200°C, 400°F, Gas Mark 6

450g/1lb potatoes
salt and pepper
2 tablespoons milk, warmed

25g/1oz butter
1 egg, beaten

Cook the potatoes in boiling salted water for about 20 minutes. Drain and return to the pan to dry off. Sieve the potatoes and add the milk and butter. Beat in the egg and seasoning. Using a piping bag fitted with a large rosette nozzle, pipe 8 mounds on to a greased baking sheet. Bake in a moderately hot oven for 30 minutes or until golden brown.

Baked or Jacket Potatoes

9 exchanges per recipe
Serves 4

Cooking time 1 hour
Oven temperature Moderately Hot
200°C, 400°F, Gas Mark 6

4 175-g/6-oz potatoes
little oil
salt
25g/1oz butter

Optional garnish
2 tablespoons soured cream
1 teaspoon chopped chives

Scrub the potatoes and dry well. Prick thoroughly with a fork. Rub with cooking oil and roll in salt. Place on a baking sheet and bake in a moderately hot oven for about 1 hour or until cooked. Cut a cross in the top of each potato, squeeze open and add a knob of butter and the soured cream mixed with chives.

Sauté Potatoes

6 exchanges per recipe
Serves 4

Cooking time about 25 minutes

450g/1lb potatoes
1 tablespoon oil
25g/1oz butter

salt and pepper
1 tablespoon chopped fresh
  parsley

Scrub the potatoes but do not peel. Cook in boiling salted water for about 15 minutes until just tender. Drain and peel when cool enough to handle. Cut in chunks, not slices. Heat the oil and butter in a frying pan. Add the still warm potatoes and fry, tossing occasionally, until they are brown and crisp. There should be no fat left in the pan. Sprinkle with seasoning and parsley and serve at once.

Gratiné Potatoes

8 exchanges per recipe
Serves 4

Cooking time 55 minutes
Oven temperature Cool 150°C,
300°F, Gas Mark 2

450g/1lb potatoes
4 onions, finely sliced
salt and pepper
150ml/¼ pint milk

75g/3oz butter
2 egg yolks
4½ tablespoons double cream
25g/1oz fresh breadcrumbs

Slice the potatoes 2mm/$\frac{1}{10}$inch thin. Simmer with the onions in the seasoned milk with 2oz/50g of the butter added for 10 minutes. Beat the egg yolks with the cream and strain in any milk that has not been absorbed by the potatoes. Transfer the potatoes and onions to a buttered ovenproof dish and pour over the egg and cream mixture. Sprinkle with breadcrumbs and dot with the remaining butter. Bake in a cool oven for 45 minutes.

Margot's Potatoes

8 exchanges per recipe
Serves 4

Cooking time 45 minutes
Oven temperature Moderate
180°C, 350°F, Gas Mark 4

675g/1½lb potatoes
2 onions, sliced
50g/2oz butter

6 anchovy fillets, chopped
300ml/½ pint single cream
25g/1oz breadcrumbs

Boil the potatoes in salted water for 15 minutes. Drain. Fry the onion in 25g/1oz of the butter until soft. Slice the cooked potatoes and arrange in layers with the anchovy and onion in a shallow ovenproof dish. Pour over the cream, sprinkle with breadcrumbs and dot with the remaining butter. Bake in a moderate oven for about 20 minutes.

Pommes Anna

6 exchanges per recipe
Serves 4

Cooking time 1 hour
Oven temperature Moderately Hot
190°C, 375°F, Gas Mark 5

450g/1lb potatoes
50g/2oz butter

salt and pepper

Slice the potatoes thinly and pat dry. Melt half the butter in a shallow cake tin or an iron frying pan which can be placed in the oven. Arrange the potato slices overlapping in a neat circle over the base, then fill up the pan with layers of potato slices, seasoning between each layer. Spoon over the remaining butter and cover with a piece of greaseproof paper or foil. Cook on top of the cooker for about 5 minutes just long enough to colour the potato circle. Transfer to a moderately hot oven and cook for 1 hour. Turn out on to a plate.

SALADS

Mixed Green Salad

Serves 4

1 bunch watercress
1 bunch spring onions
1 Cos lettuce

½ green pepper
vinaigrette dressing (see page 59)

Cut the prepared vegetables into bite-sized pieces and toss in a highly seasoned vinaigrette dressing.

Avocado-Bacon Salad

Serves 4

Cooking time 8 minutes

1 Cos lettuce
100g/4oz streaky bacon
1 bunch spring onions

2 avocados
vinaigrette dressing (see page 59)

Wash the lettuce and tear into 5-cm/2-inch pieces. Fry the bacon until crisp. Drain on kitchen paper. Crumble. Place the lettuce in a shallow bowl, cut the spring onions on to it. Add the thinly sliced avocado and bacon to the salad. Dress with vinaigrette and serve at once.

Green Salad with Beetroot and Walnuts

2 exchanges per recipe
Serves 4

225g/8oz chicory
1 lettuce (or 2 bunches
    watercress, or endive or
    Chinese cabbage)

1 large beetroot, cooked and diced
50g/2oz walnuts, chopped
vinaigrette dressing (see page 59)

Wash and dry the green salad vegetables. Combine with the beetroot and walnuts and toss in the vinaigrette dressing just before serving.

Mushroom Salad

Serves 4

450g/1lb tiny button
  mushrooms
2 tablespoons lemon juice
6 tablespoons olive oil

1 teaspoon crushed coriander
  seeds
few tarragon leaves, chopped

Combine the ingredients together just before serving.

Cucumber and Mint Salad

Serves 4

1 cucumber
salt
1 teaspoon chopped fresh
  mint

vinaigrette dressing
  (see page 59)

Slice the unpeeled cucumber very thinly. Spread the slices on a plate
and sprinkle with salt. Leave for 30 minutes, then drain off the liquid.
Mix the mint into the dressing and spoon over the cucumber.

Cole Slaw Salad

3 exchanges per recipe
Serves 4

450g/1lb hard white cabbage,
  shredded
1 dessert apple, unpeeled
  and sliced
25g/1oz seedless raisins
25g/1oz walnuts, chopped

2 sticks of celery, sliced
4 tablespoons mayonnaise
  (see page 57)
  or boiled dressing
  (see page 59)

Combine the salad ingredients together 30 minutes before serving.

Hot Cole Slaw Salad

Serves 4   *Cooking time 1 minute*

675g/1½lb hard white
  cabbage, shredded
1 teaspoon salt
¼ teaspoon black pepper

1 teaspoon dill seed
150ml/¼ pint soured cream
2 tablespoons wine vinegar

Immerse the shredded cabbage in boiling water for 1 minute. Mix all the other ingredients together. Drain the cabbage throughly. Dress with the soured cream mixture and serve at once.

Broad Bean Salad

3 exchanges per recipe   *Cooking time about 20 minutes*
Serves 4

450g/1lb podded broad beans
2-3 spring onions, chopped
½ teaspoon poppy seeds

vinaigrette dressing
  (see page 59)

Cook the broad beans in boiling salted water until tender. Drain and cool. Add the chopped spring onions and poppy seeds to the vinaigrette dressing. Spoon over the beans.

Tomato, Onion and Pepper Salad

Serves 4

4 large tomatoes
1 onion, preferably Spanish
1 large green pepper

1 teaspoon chopped mixed
  herbs
vinaigrette dressing
  (see page 59)

Peel the tomatoes and cut them into quarters. Remove the cores. Peel and slice the onion very finely. Cut the pepper in half, remove the seeds and slice finely. Mix the herbs into the vinaigrette dressing. Toss the salad ingredients together in the dressing.

Cucumber Yogurt Salad

1 exchange per recipe
Serves 4

1 large cucumber
salt
150ml/¼ pint natural yogurt

ground black pepper
chopped chives

Grate the unpeeled cucumber. Add salt and leave to stand for 30 minutes. Drain thoroughly. Just before serving, mix with the yogurt, black pepper and chives.

Fennel and Lemon Salad

Serves 4

Cooking time 5 minutes

2-3 heads fennel
2 lemons

vinaigrette dressing made with
lemon juice (see page 59)

Wash and trim the fennel. Cut in half and then slice very finely across the stem. Pare off a little of the lemon zest with a potato peeler and shred finely, or use a zester. Blanch in a little boiling water and drain. Set aside for garnish. Cut the skin and pith from the lemons and then remove each segment free of membrane. Mix with the fennel and vinaigrette dressing. Sprinkle with the lemon zest.

Batavia and Apple Salad

2 exchanges per serving
Serves 4

1 head of Batavia lettuce
2 100-g/4-oz dessert apples

squeeze of lemon juice
vinaigrette dressing (see page 59)

Wash, dry and shred the lettuce. Wash the apples but do not peel. Quarter, core and slice them, sprinkle with lemon juice. Just before serving, toss the lettuce and apple in the vinaigrette dressing.

Batavia and Walnut Salad   To make the above salad *exchange-free*, substitute 50g/2oz chopped walnuts for the apple and use walnut oil.

Bean Sprout Salad

Serves 4   *Cooking time 1 minute*

225g/8oz bean sprouts
2 sticks of celery, sliced
50g/2oz walnuts, chopped
½ teaspoon caraway seeds

vinaigrette dressing made with
 lemon juice (see page 59)
4 lettuce leaves

Cook the bean sprouts in boiling water for 1 minute. Drain; refresh with cold water. Mix the sprouts, celery, walnuts and caraway seeds with the dressing and spoon on to the bed of lettuce leaves.

Mushroom and Broad Bean Salad

1½ exchanges per recipe
Serves 4

225g/8oz button mushrooms
vinaigrette dressing (see page 59)

½ teaspoon chopped fresh dill or
 parsley
225g/8oz cooked broad beans

Wipe the mushrooms and slice thinly. Mix the dressing with the dill or parsley and add to the mushrooms and cooked broad beans. Toss well.

Carrot and Sultana Salad

5 exchanges per recipe
Serves 4

450g/1lb carrots
50g/2oz sultanas
1 teaspoon crushed coriander
 seeds
1 teaspoon Dijon mustard

4 tablespoons vinaigrette dressing
 (see page 59)
2 tablespoons chopped fresh
 parsley

Peel the carrots and cut into julienne (matchstick) strips or grate. Mix with the sultanas and coriander seeds. Add the Dijon mustard to the vinaigrette dressing and pour over the salad. Refrigerate overnight. Serve sprinkled generously with chopped parsley.

Cauliflower and Caper Salad

Serves 4   *Cooking time 2 minutes (optional)*

1 medium cauliflower
2 tablespoons wine vinegar
8 tablespoons olive oil
3 cloves garlic, crushed

175g/6oz capers
salt and pepper
1 tablespoon chopped fresh
  parsley

Cut the cauliflower into tiny florets and use raw, or blanch in boiling salted water for 2 minutes. Combine the remaining ingredients and marinate the cauliflower in this for at least 30 minutes before serving.

Watercress and Orange Salad

2 exchanges per recipe
Serves 4

2-3 bunches watercress   vinaigrette dressing (see page 59)
2 large oranges

Wash and pick over the watercress. Cut the skin and pith from the oranges; using a sharp knife, work carefully round the orange to leave the flesh bare. Cut the segments free from the membrane. Just before serving, toss the oranges and watercress in the vinaigrette dressing.

Tomato Salad

Serves 4

6 large tomatoes   1 teaspoon chopped fresh basil
vinaigrette dressing (see page 59)

Peel the tomatoes and slice thinly. Arrange on a plate. Spoon over the vinaigrette dressing and sprinkle with basil. Chill before serving.

SAUCES, DRESSINGS AND SAVOURY BUTTERS

White Sauce

3 exchanges per recipe
Makes scant 300ml/½ pint

Cooking time 10 minutes

25g/1oz butter
20g/¾oz plain flour

200ml/⅓ pint cold milk
salt and pepper

Melt the butter in a pan. Add the flour and cook for 1-2 minutes, stirring. Remove from the heat and blend in the milk, stir until smooth. Return to the heat and, stirring all the time, bring to the boil. Allow to boil thoroughly for at least 1 minute. Add salt and pepper to taste.

Béchamel sauce   Infuse the milk with a slice of onion, slice of carrot and a bouquet garni (see page 177). Allow to cool a little before straining and blending.

Cheese sauce   Add 50g/2oz grated strong cheese and ½ teaspoon Dijon mustard after the sauce has boiled. Do not reboil.

Hollandaise Sauce

Serves 4   *Cooking time about 15 minutes*

2 egg yolks
1 teaspoon lemon juice or wine
  vinegar

salt and pepper
175g/6oz butter, cut in small
  pieces

Beat the egg yolks with the lemon juice or wine vinegar and seasoning in a small bowl. Stand the bowl over a pan of hot, but not boiling, water. Add the pieces of butter, one at a time, waiting until the first is absorbed before adding the next. Use a fork or a small whisk to mix. When all the butter is absorbed, test for seasoning and add more lemon juice or vinegar if necessary. This sauce is best made just before it is needed. Keep warm over hot water but do not overheat.

Yogurt

3 exchanges per recipe
Makes 600ml/1 pint

Home-made yogurt is easy to make and cheaper than shop-bought.

600ml/1 pint milk   1 tablespoon natural yogurt

Bring the milk to the boil in an enamel or stainless steel pan. Stir the milk as it heats to prevent a skin forming. If it does form a skin later, remove it. Allow the milk to cool to blood heat. Beat the yogurt until smooth in a large bowl. Add a little milk from the pan and then stir in the remainder. Cover the bowl with foil and put in a warm place such as the airing cupboard or above the hot water tank. Leave without disturbing for at least 8 hours, or overnight. Refrigerate when it has reached the consistency required. Store in a tightly covered container. It will keep in the refrigerator for about a week. Reserve a little to serve as starter for the next batch.

Béarnaise Sauce

Serves 4   *Cooking time about 15 minutes*

4 tablespoons dry white wine
2 tablespoons tarragon
   vinegar
4 spring onions, finely
   chopped
2 egg yolks

175g/6oz butter, cut in small
   pieces
salt and pepper
lemon juice
4-6 tarragon leaves

Put the wine, vinegar and spring onions into a small pan and boil rapidly until no more than 1½ tablespoons of liquid remain in the pan. Quickly add two drops of water – this will prevent further evaporation. Beat the egg yolks with this liquid in a small bowl. Stand the bowl over a pan of hot, but not boiling, water. Add the pieces of butter one at a time, waiting until the first is absorbed before adding the next. Use a fork or small whisk to mix. When all the butter is absorbed, test for seasoning. The addition of a few drops of lemon juice may be required. Finish the sauce by snipping in fresh tarragon leaves. This sauce is best made just before it is needed. It may be kept warm over hot water but must not be overheated.

Mayonnaise

1-2 egg yolks
1 teaspoon wine vinegar or
   lemon juice
pinch salt

pinch pepper
¼ teaspoon dry or Dijon
   mustard
300ml/½ pint olive oil

Both the egg yolks and oil should be at room temperature. Secure the bowl by twisting a damp cloth around the base. Beat the egg yolks with the vinegar or lemon juice, seasoning and mustard. Beat in the oil, drop by drop, until the mixture thickens. Add the rest of the oil in a steady stream, beating thoroughly to ensure that it is absorbed. (Mayonnaise may also be made using an electric hand beater or in a blender.) Adjust the seasoning. For a lighter mayonnaise and to improve its keeping, add a few drops of boiling water to the finished sauce.

Note   If the sauce should fail to thicken, add a teaspoon of boiling water. If that fails, start again with another egg yolk and more seasoning in another bowl. Drip the curdled mixture on to the new egg yolk and increase the oil. The resulting surplus can be stored in a cool place, *not the refrigerator*, for several days.

Rémoulade sauce: To 300ml/½ pint classic mayonnaise add 1 teaspoon Dijon mustard, 2 teaspoons chopped gherkins, 2 teaspoons chopped capers, 1 teaspoon chopped fresh parsley, tarragon and chervil mixed.

Tartare sauce: Use cooked egg yolks in place of raw for the mayonnaise. Add finely chopped onions and chives to the sauce.

Cheese mayonnaise: To half quantity of mayonnaise, add 2 tablespoons grated Gruyère or fresh Parmesan. When not available, use Cheddar. You may need to use slightly more Cheddar. Taste for flavour.

Yogurt mayonnaise: Mix equal quantities of mayonnaise and natural yogurt (see page 56), adding extra salt, lemon juice and crushed garlic or chopped mixed herbs or curry powder to taste. Excellent with cold fish (*150ml/¼ pint yogurt equals 1 exchange*).

Bread Sauce

7 exchanges per recipe

Cooking time 8 minutes

200ml/⅓ pint milk
1 small onion, sliced
2 cloves
1 small piece of bay leaf

75g/3oz fresh breadcrumbs
15g/½oz butter
salt and pepper

Heat the milk with the onion, cloves and bay leaf until boiling. Remove from the heat and leave to infuse. Strain. Return to the pan and add the breadcrumbs. Simmer for 2-3 minutes or until thick and creamy, stirring. Finally, add the butter and seasoning.

Vinaigrette Dressing

Serves 4

1 tablespoon wine vinegar
3-5 tablespoons olive oil,
   according to taste

salt and pepper
pinch dry mustard or ½ teaspoon
   Dijon

Combine the ingredients in a wide necked screw topped jar and shake vigorously. Shake again just before use. To save time, make a larger quantity and store it in the jar.

The dressing may be varied with the following additions: Fresh herbs, dried herbs, curry powder or paste, tomato juice or purée, carraway seeds, lemon juice, grapefruit or lime juice may be used in place of vinegar. The sauce may be finished with 1 tablespoon soured cream and/or a little crushed garlic.

Boiled Dressing

2 exchanges per recipe

Cooking time about 12 minutes

25g/1oz butter
15g/½oz flour
¼ teaspoon salt
½ teaspoon dry mustard
pinch cayenne pepper

150ml/¼ pint milk
1 egg, beaten
2 tablespoons cider vinegar
1 tablespoon single cream

Melt the butter and sift in the dry ingredients. Whisk in the milk, egg and vinegar and cook over the heat until boiling, stirring. Simmer for a few minutes. Cool and store in an airtight container. Add the cream just before use.

Spicy Marinade

Use for chicken and lamb pieces to be grilled. Marinade in this mixture overnight. May also be added to cooked potatoes before they are sautéed.

1 exchange per recipe   *Cooking time 5 minutes*

2 teaspoons fennel seeds   150ml/¼ pint natural yogurt
1 teaspoon ground coriander   (see page 56)
                                            1 clove garlic, crushed

Dry fry the spices for 5 minutes, shaking the pan continuously to prevent burning. Grind the spices and mix into the yogurt. Stir in the crushed garlic.

Cucumber Relish

1 cucumber, peeled and sliced   1 tablespoon salt
1 tablespoon boiling water   2 artificial sweetener tablets
4 tablespoons wine vinegar

Combine the ingredients and leave for 1 hour. Drain. The cucumber will be seasoned but retain its bite. The liquid can be saved for another batch.

Gravy

2 exchanges per recipe   *Cooking time about 8 minutes*
Makes 300ml/½ pint

2 tablespoons dripping   salt and pepper
25g/1oz flour   gravy browning
300ml/½ pint bone stock
  (see page 61)

Melt the dripping, add the flour and cook for 1 minute or so until the flour begins to colour. Add the stock and bring to the boil. Add seasoning and gravy browning to make a rich brown colour.

Note Roast beef is best cooked in fresh beef dripping. Buy fresh beef fat from the butcher, place it in a roasting tin and render it in a moderate oven. Check every 15 minutes and strain off the liquid fat into a bowl.

Bone Stock

Cooking time 30 minutes

1kg/2lb marrow bones
generous litre/2 pints water
2 onions, quartered
2 carrots, quartered

2 sticks of celery, halved
6 peppercorns
½ teaspoon salt

Place the bones in a pressure cooker, cover with cold water, bring to the boil and skim off the scum which forms. Add the remaining ingredients. Put the lid on the cooker, bring to high pressure and cook for 30 minutes. Allow the pressure to reduce at room temperature. Strain and cool. The stock will keep for 4 days in the refrigerator.

Note To make chicken stock, use the bones from a roasted chicken. The giblets may also be used but exclude the liver. You may use two pieces of boiling fowl instead of a chicken carcass but this method is both more expensive and less tasty.

SAVOURY BUTTERS

All these butters may be made in advance. Put the prepared butter into a small pot or pots. Smooth the tops and place in the refrigerator to harden. They may be used either to cook the food or brought to the table and served as an accompaniment.

Anchovy Butter

4 anchovy fillets
2 tablespoons milk

50g/2oz butter, creamed
black pepper

Soak the anchovies in the milk for 30 minutes to remove excess salt. Drain and pound in a mortar. Beat into the butter and add the pepper.

Garlic Butter

4 cloves garlic
50g/2oz butter, creamed

salt and pepper
squeeze of lemon juice

Blanch the garlic in boiling water for 5 minutes. Crush in a garlic press. Add to the butter and season with salt and pepper. Add lemon juice to taste. Mix well.

Lemon Butter

grated rind of 1 lemon
1 teaspoon lemon juice

50g/2oz butter, creamed
salt and pepper

Beat the lemon rind and juice into the butter and season to taste.

Parsley or Herb Butter

Add 1 teaspoon chopped fresh parsley or herbs to the lemon butter recipe above.

Mustard Butter

2 teaspoons Dijon mustard

50g/2oz butter, creamed

Beat the mustard into the butter.

Orange Butter

50g/2oz butter, creamed
grated rind of 1 orange
2 teaspoons orange juice

½ teaspoon paprika pepper
salt

Beat all the ingredients together.

Curry Butter

100g/4oz butter, softened
1 teaspoon curry powder

½ teaspoon lemon juice
salt

Mix all the ingredients together. Use for spreading in egg, chicken and ham sandwiches.

Apple Sauce

2 exchanges per recipe
Serves 4

Cooking time 10 minutes

225g/8oz cooking apples
4 tablespoons water
strip of lemon rind

15g/½oz butter
artificial sweetener (optional)

Wash the apples, chop roughly and put in a pan with the water and lemon rind. Cover and cook to a pulp. Rub through a sieve. Return the apple purée to the rinsed out pan, add the butter and artificial sweetener, if liked.

Melba Sauce

1 exchange per recipe
Serves 4

175g/6oz fresh or frozen
   raspberries

2 tablespoons diabetic
   raspberry jam

Sieve the raspberries and stir into the jam.

Cream Sauce

½ exchange per recipe　　　　　　*Cooking time 5 minutes*

100g/4oz unsalted butter　　　　　　½ teaspoon gelatine
6 tablespoons milk　　　　　　　　　4 drops vanilla essence

Heat the butter and milk gently until the butter is melted. Pour into a
blender and liquidise with the gelatine for 1 minute. Add the essence.
Leave to cool. Good served with apple compote.

Seasoned Flour

4 exchanges per recipe

50g/2oz plain flour　　　　　　　　　¼ teaspoon freshly ground black
1½ teaspoons dry mustard　　　　　　　pepper
1 teaspoon salt

Sift the ingredients together and store in an airtight jar. Proportions may
be varied to suit individual tastes.

BAKING

Shortcrust Pastry

16 exchanges per recipe

225g/8oz plain flour, white or
  wholemeal
pinch salt

50g/2oz butter
50g/2oz lard
3 tablespoons iced water

Sift the flour with the salt into a mixing bowl. Cut in the fats, then rub
the fats into the flour until the mixture resembles breadcrumbs. Add the
water quickly and mix to a dough using a knife. The pastry dough
should be damp but not sticky. Wrap in greaseproof paper and chill for
about 15 minutes. Use as directed in the recipe. Wholewheat pastry will
bake a little harder than white.

Note　I like a *very* short pastry – particularly for the Turkish meat
pasties and other pastry dishes that are to constitute the main feature of a
meal. To make *very* short pastry you simply alter the proportions of fat
to flour: the more fat the shorter the result.
175g/6oz plain flour, 50g/2oz butter, 50g/2oz lard would be
appropriate for the Turkish meat pasties (see page 111) and the whole
quantity contains *12 exchanges*.

Suet Crust Pastry

16 exchanges per recipe

225g/8oz self-raising flour
pinch salt

100g/4oz shredded suet
cold water to mix

Sift the flour with the salt into a bowl. Add the suet and mix thoroughly.
Add enough cold water to give a soft but not sticky dough. Use at once as
directed.

Rough Puff Pastry

This is a quick method suitable for sausage rolls, meat pie toppings etc.

16 exchanges per recipe

225g/8oz plain flour
pinch salt

175g/6oz block margarine
cold water to mix

Sift the flour into a bowl with the salt. Take the margarine from the refrigerator and grate quickly into the flour, using the coarsest side of the grater. It helps to dip the block of margarine into the flour several times. Use the fingers to shake the flour through the grated margarine. Add enough water to bind. It will be a little stickier than shortcrust and will look rough. Flour the hands and pat into a rectangle. Wrap in greaseproof paper and chill for at least 1 hour. Roll out and use as directed.

Choux Pastry

6 exchanges per recipe

75g/3oz plain flour
pinch salt
50g/2oz butter or margarine

150ml/¼ pint water
2 (size 4/medium) eggs

Sift the flour with the salt on to a piece of stiff paper. Melt the butter or margarine in a medium size pan. Add the water and bring to the boil. Add all the flour immediately. Remove from the heat and beat until the mixture forms a smooth paste which leaves the sides of the pan. Beat the eggs in a bowl and add a spoonful at a time, beating well after each addition. Continue until all the egg is absorbed. Beat thoroughly. The mixture is now ready to be used as directed.

Ground Almond Pastry

7 exchanges per recipe   *Cooking time 15-25 minutes*
Oven temperature Moderately Hot 190°C, 375°F, Gas Mark 5

75g/3oz plain flour   75g/3oz butter
75g/3oz ground almonds   1 tablespoon iced water

Sift the flour into a bowl and add the ground almonds. Rub in the butter until the mixture resembles fine breadcrumbs. Combine the ingredients with the iced water. Roll into a ball and place in greaseproof paper in the refrigerator for at least 1 hour before using. Use as ordinary shortcrust pastry. Bake in a moderately hot oven for 15-25 minutes.

Note   This pastry tastes particularly good if it is slightly over-cooked. Cooking time 15-25 minutes depending on the degree of brownness you like. The quantity makes 14 tartlet shells (*2 per exchange*).

White Custard

1 exchange per recipe   *Cooking time 5 minutes*
Serves 2

2 egg whites, lightly whisked   ½ teaspoon lemon, rose, coffee
150ml/¼ pint milk   or vanilla essence
2 artificial sweetener tablets

Pour the lightly whisked egg whites and milk into a saucepan and bring to the boil. Simmer, stirring, for 3 minutes. Add the artificial sweetener, pour into a bowl and allow to cool. Add the flavouring essence of your choice.

Basic Brown or White Bread

38 exchanges per recipe　　　　　*Cooking time 40 minutes*
Oven temperature Hot 230°C, 450°F, Gas Mark 8, then Moderately Hot
*　200°C, 400°F, Gas Mark 6 for 20 minutes*
Makes 1 1-kg/2-lb loaf

575g/1¼lb strong white flour or　　15g/½oz fresh yeast or 8g/¼oz
　wholemeal flour or a mixture　　　dried yeast
　in any proportion　　　　　　　about 350ml/12fl oz tepid water
20g/¾oz salt

Warm the flour in a large ovenproof bowl in a cool oven for a few
minutes. Mix in the salt. Put the yeast in a cup and cover with a little of
the tepid water and leave to dissolve and froth. This may take 10
minutes. Mix the yeast into the flour with enough water to make a soft
elastic dough. White flour will absorb more than wholemeal. Mix
vigorously until the dough forms a smooth ball. Cover the bowl with a
piece of oiled polythene or oil the dough and cover with a damp tea towel.
Leave at room temperature to rise until doubled in size. It is not
necessary to find a specially warm place. Just keep it out of a draught.
When risen, knock the dough down and knead thoroughly for 3–4
minutes. Pat out to a large oblong, roll up and drop into a greased 1-
kg/2-lb bread tin. Leave to prove for another 45 minutes or until the
dough reaches the top of the tin. Bake in a hot oven for 20 minutes, then
reduce the heat to moderately hot for a further 20 minutes. When ready,
the loaf should sound hollow when tapped on the base. Cool on a wire
rack before storing. Cut into 19 slices. *One slice equals 2 exchanges.*

Oatcakes

16 exchanges per recipe
Makes 16

Cooking time 20 minutes
Oven temperature Moderate
160°C, 325°F, Gas Mark 3

225g/8oz medium oatmeal
¼ teaspoon bicarbonate of soda
¼ teaspoon salt
pinch cinnamon

15g/½oz bacon fat, lard, butter
  or margarine
4 tablespoons boiling water

Mix the dry ingredients and make a well in the centre. Melt the fat in the water and pour into the oatmeal. Mix to a sticky dough and divide in two. Roll out each piece into a neat circle as thin as possible. Cut across into eight triangles. Bake on a dry baking sheet in a moderate oven for 20 minutes or until crisp and lightly browned.

Cheese and Bacon Scones

18 exchanges per recipe
Makes 18

Cooking time 12-15 minutes
Oven temperature Hot 220°C,
425°F, Gas Mark 7

4 rashers streaky bacon
225g/8oz self-raising flour
½ teaspoon salt
½ teaspoon dry mustard

50g/2oz butter
100g/4oz strong Cheddar cheese,
  grated
150ml/¼ pint milk

Fry the bacon until crisp. Sift the flour, salt and mustard into a mixing bowl. Rub in the butter until the mixture resembles breadcrumbs. Crumble the bacon and add to the mixture with the cheese. Make a well in the centre and add the milk. Mix until the dough leaves the sides of the bowl clean. Knead lightly until smooth. Roll out to 5-cm/2-inch thickness and stamp out 18 rounds with a small biscuit cutter. Place on a greased baking sheet and bake in a hot oven for 12-15 minutes until golden brown.

Cornflake Biscuits

14 exchanges per recipe
Makes 14

100g/4oz cornflakes
50g/2oz sultanas
50g/2oz hazelnuts, halved and
   toasted

150g/5oz diabetic chocolate,
   melted with 1 tablespoon water

Crush the cornflakes roughly. Add the sultanas and hazelnuts. Pour over the melted chocolate and mix lightly. Place a tablespoon of the mixture into 14 paper cups.

Garlic Bread

20-g/¾oz slice of bread
   equals 1 exchange
Oven temperature Hot 230°C, 450°F, Gas Mark 8

Cooking time 10 minutes

1 French loaf
100g/4oz butter, creamed

4 cloves garlic, crushed

Slice the bread thickly to within 5mm/¼ inch of the base. Mix the butter and garlic and spread between the slices. Wrap in foil and crisp in a hot oven for 10 minutes.

Variations:
Mustard bread Replace the garlic with 1 teaspoon Dijon mustard.
Herb bread Replace the garlic with 2 teaspoons chopped fresh mixed herbs.

Note There are many occasions when it would be wasteful to heat the oven. Making a single dish is one such occasion. When I want garlic bread with a meal that otherwise does not require the oven, I make garlic butter and spread it on hot toast. This alternative is perfectly satisfactory.

EVERYDAY MENUS

MENU 1

(Illustrated on the cover)

5 exchanges per serving
Serves 4

Eggs with Watercress

Cooking time 15 minutes

4 eggs
1 bunch watercress
6 tablespoons mayonnaise
(see page 57)

2 tablespoons double cream,
whipped
salt and pepper

Boil the eggs for 15 minutes and plunge into cold water. Wash and pick the leaves from the watercress, reserving a little for garnish. Put the leaves into a blender with the mayonnaise and liquidise until the leaves are thoroughly mixed into the sauce. Arrange the quartered hard-boiled eggs on a serving dish. Add the cream and seasoning, if necessary, to the watercress sauce and spoon over the eggs. Garnish with the reserved watercress.

Moussaka

Moussaka: ½ exchange per serving
Garlic bread: 3½ exchanges per serving

Cooking time about 1¼ hours

Oven temperature Moderately Hot 200°C, 400°F, Gas Mark 6

1 aubergine
2 onions, chopped
4-6 tablespoons olive oil
100g/4oz mushrooms, sliced
450g/1lb minced beef
large pinch dried herbs
salt and pepper

1 396-g/14-oz can tomatoes
2 tablespoons tomato purée
Topping
2 eggs
1 tablespoon plain flour
150ml/¼ pint natural yogurt

72

Slice the aubergine, without peeling, sprinkle with salt and leave to drain in a colander for at least 1 hour. Fry the onions in 2 tablespoons of the oil until golden brown. Add the mushrooms and cook for 1 minute. Set aside. Rinse the aubergine slices and pat dry with kitchen paper. Fry in 2-3 tablespoons oil until golden brown on each side. Set aside. Fry the minced beef in 1 tablespoon oil, if necessary, and add the herbs. Place half of the mince mixture into a greased ovenproof dish. Cover with a layer of aubergines and a layer of onions and mushrooms. Sprinkle with seasoning. Repeat with the remaining meat and vegetables. Liquidise the canned tomatoes with the tomato purée and pour over the dish. Cook, uncovered, in a moderately hot oven for 35 minutes.

Beat the eggs with the flour, yogurt, salt and pepper. Pour over the meat and vegetables. Return to the oven and cook for a further 15 minutes. Serve with Garlic bread — *3½ exchanges per serving* (see page 70) and Mixed green salad (see page 49).

Gooseberry Fool

1 exchange per serving   *Cooking time about 15 minutes*

450g/1lb dessert gooseberries   artificial sweetener to taste
1½ tablespoons water   150ml/¼ pint double cream,
spray of elderflowers (optional)   lightly whipped

Wash the fruit and put in a pan with the water. Add a spray of elderflowers, if available. Simmer very slowly until the fruit is soft, this will take about 15 minutes. Remove the elderflowers, if used. Sieve the fruit. While the mixture is hot, add the artificial sweetener to taste. Leave to cool. When cold, fold in the lightly whipped cream. If liked, decorate with small rosettes of cream.

MENU 2

4 exchanges per serving
Serves 4

Carrot and Ginger Salad

½ exchange per serving   *Cooking time 8-10 minutes*

450g/1lb young carrots
4 tablespoons olive oil
10-cm/4-inch piece fresh ginger,
   grated

vinaigrette dressing (see page 59)
chopped fresh parsley

Cut the carrots into diagonal slices. Put the olive oil in a frying pan and cook the ginger gently for 1 minute. Add the carrots and turn them in the oil for 2 minutes. Pour over boiling water to cover and cook until just soft, approximately 5 minutes depending upon the thickness of the slices. Cool in the liquid. Dress with the vinaigrette and sprinkle with plenty of chopped parsley.

For a 5-exchange menu serve with Herb bread – 1 exchange per serving (see page 70).

Oxtail Stew

1½ exchange per serving   *Cooking time about 3 hours,*
                                  next day 1 hour

Oven temperature Moderate 160°C, 325°F, Gas Mark 3

1kg/2lb oxtail, jointed
1 tablespoon dripping
1 onion, sliced
1 carrot, sliced
1 stick celery, sliced

salt and pepper
1 bay leaf
450g/1lb potatoes, cut in thick
   slices

Trim any excess fat from the pieces of oxtail. Melt the dripping in a frying pan and fry the oxtail until brown. Place in a large ovenproof casserole. Fry the vegetables until light brown and add to the oxtail. Add enough water to just cover the meat, season and add the bay leaf. Cook in a moderate oven for 3 hours. Allow to cool overnight. Next day, remove the excess fat from the casserole. Cover with a layer of sliced potatoes, adjust the seasoning and cook for 1 hour in a moderate oven or until the potatoes are cooked.

Curd Cheese and Orange Tarts

2 exchanges per serving *Cooking time 20 minutes*
Oven temperature Moderately Hot 190°C, 375°F, Gas Mark 5

ground almond pastry
  (see page 67)
Filling
100g/4oz curd cheese

4 tablespoons double cream
2 tablespoons currants
grated rind of 2 oranges

Make the pastry, roll out and cut 16 small circles. Use to line a patty tin and bake blind in a moderately hot oven for 20 minutes. Leave to cool. Mix the ingredients for the filling and fill the tart shells just before serving. Allow 4 tarts per person.

MENU 3

4 exchanges per serving
Serves 2

Balkan Soup

½ exchange per serving

150ml/¼ pint chicken stock
150ml/¼ pint home-made yogurt
(see page 56)
1 tablespoon lemon juice
1 clove garlic, crushed

¼ cucumber, unpeeled and
grated
salt and pepper
300ml/½ pint iced water
chopped fresh mint to garnish

Combine the stock, yogurt, lemon juice, garlic and cucumber. Season well. Add the water slowly — you may not need the whole quantity, depending on the consistency you prefer. Test again for seasoning. Garnish with chopped mint.

Spanish Omelette

Brown bread: 3½ exchanges
per serving

Cooking time 20 minutes

4 eggs
salt and pepper
1 tablespoon olive oil
Filling
1 small onion, sliced
1 100-g/4-oz potato, diced

1 small green pepper, chopped
1 clove garlic, crushed
2 tomatoes, peeled and quartered
100g/4oz cooked ham, diced
4 stuffed green olives, sliced
chopped fresh parsley to garnish

Beat the eggs with the seasoning. Heat the oil in an omelette pan. Add the onion and potato and fry gently until soft and brown. Add the other filling ingredients and cook for a further 3 minutes. Pour in the egg mixture and cook quickly for about 3 minutes until lightly browned on the under side. Place under a hot grill to brown the top. Sprinkle with parsley and serve at once with brown bread and butter *(3½ exchanges per serving)*.

For a 5-exchange menu serve with extra brown bread and butter – 1 exchange.

Lemon Cream

Cooking time 5-10 minutes

rind and juice of 1 lemon
2 egg yolks
25g/1oz butter

artificial sweetener to taste
150ml/¼ pint double cream, whipped

Put the finely grated rind and juice of the lemon into a bowl with the egg yolks and butter. Place the bowl over a pan of simmering water. Cook, stirring continually, until thickened. Do not allow the mixture to boil. Add the sweetener to taste and leave to cool. Fold the lemon mixture into the whipped cream. Divide between 2 wine glasses.

MENU 4

5 exchanges per serving
Serves 4

Cheese Patties

2 exchanges per serving   *Cooking time about 20 minutes*
Oven temperature Hot 230°C, 450°F, Gas Mark 8

1 212-g/7½-oz packet frozen
  puff pastry
Filling
50g/2oz mushrooms, finely
  chopped
15g/½oz butter

225g/8oz curd cheese
3 tablespoons finely chopped
  fresh parsley
salt and pepper
2 egg yolks

Sauté the mushrooms in the butter for 2 minutes. Allow to cool. Mix the curd cheese with the parsley, seasoning, 1 egg yolk and mushrooms. Roll out the pastry very thinly and cut into circles. Put a teaspoon of filling in each circle and seal the pastry edges with cold water. Place on a baking sheet and glaze with the remaining beaten egg yolk. Bake in a hot oven for 15 minutes.

Baked Mackerel with Watercress and Anchovy Butter

Potato crisps: 2 exchanges   *Cooking time 15 minutes*
   per serving
Oven temperature Moderate 180°C, 350°F, Gas Mark 4

1 bunch of watercress   squeeze of lemon juice
50g/2oz butter, softened   *To garnish*
1 teaspoon anchovy essence   watercress sprigs
4 medium mackerel, filleted   lemon wedges
salt and pepper

First make the savoury butter. Chop the watercress leaves very finely. Add to the softened butter with the anchovy essence. Form into a roll in a piece of greaseproof paper and chill. Butter an ovenproof dish and place the fillets of mackerel skin side down. Sprinkle with salt and pepper and a squeeze of lemon juice. Bake in a moderate oven for 15 minutes. Cut the roll of savoury butter into pats and place on the fillets of fish just before serving. Garnish with watercress sprigs and lemon wedges. Serve with potato crisps (*2 exchanges per serving*).

Yogurt Mousse

1 exchange per serving

450ml/¾ pint thick fruit purée,   150ml/¼ pint home-made yogurt
   made from your preferred fruit   (see page 56)
   (see Note)   2 egg whites

Combine the fruit purée and yogurt. Whisk the egg whites stiffly and fold into the mixture. Pour into wine glasses. Chill before serving.

Note The fruit purée must contain no more than *3 exchanges*.

MENU 5

Courgette Soup

Cooking time 25 minutes

25g/1oz butter
1 onion, chopped
450g/1lb courgettes, sliced
900ml/1½ pints chicken stock
  or use bouillon cubes

salt and pepper
150ml/¼ pint milk
2 tablespoons natural yogurt
  to garnish

Melt the butter in a pan, add the onion and fry without browning until soft. Add the courgettes, stock and seasoning. Simmer for 20 minutes or until the courgettes are tender. Allow to cool slightly. Liquidise in a blender with the milk. Adjust the seasoning. Serve with a spoonful of yogurt in each bowl.

Highland Herrings

Highland herrings:
  ½ *exchange per serving*
Watercress and orange salad:
  ½ *exchange per serving*

Cooking time 10 minutes

2 herrings
6 tablespoons milk
40g/1½oz dry medium oatmeal

salt and pepper
25g/1oz butter

Ask the fishmonger to remove the heads and backbones from the fish. Wash the herrings and pat dry with kitchen paper. Put the milk in a shallow dish and the oatmeal with salt and pepper in another. Dip the fish first in the milk and then in the oatmeal. Place on a greased grill pan, cut side up. Dot with butter and grill for about 5 minutes, then turn over and grill for a further 5 minutes. Serve with half quantity Watercress and orange salad – *½ exchange per serving* (see page 54).

Scones with Clotted Cream and Jam

4 exchanges per serving   *Cooking time 10 minutes*
Makes 6 scones
Oven temperature Hot 220°C, 425°F, Gas Mark 8

100g/4oz flour   ½ teaspoon bicarbonate of soda
pinch salt   25g/1oz butter
1 teaspoon cream of tartar   3-4 tablespoons milk

Sift the flour with the salt, cream of tartar and bicarbonate of soda. Rub in the butter. Add enough milk to make a soft dough, knead lightly and quickly until smooth. Roll out to 2cm/¾ inch thick. Cut into 6 rounds using a 5-cm/2-inch cutter. Brush with milk. Bake in a hot oven for about 10 minutes until well risen and a light brown. Cool on a wire rack. Serve with clotted cream and diabetic jam (see page 21).

MENU 6

Fish Chowder

1¾ exchanges per serving *Cooking time 35 minutes*

Stock
fish head, tail etc.
1 onion, sliced
1 carrot, sliced
1 stick of celery, sliced
generous 1 litre/2 pints water
Chowder
2 onions, chopped
25g/1oz bacon fat

450g/1lb potatoes, sliced
450g/1lb firm white fish, cut in
  steaks
175ml/6fl oz milk
1 bay leaf
large pinch saffron
salt and pepper
chopped fresh parsley
  to garnish

To make the stock, place all the fish trimmings in a pan with the vegetables and water. Bring to the boil and simmer for 20 minutes. Strain.

Meanwhile, fry the onions in the bacon fat in a large pan until transparent. Boil the potatoes separately in water for 5 minutes. Add to the onions with the fish, fish stock, milk, bay leaf, saffron and seasoning. Simmer for 15 minutes. Serve in individual bowls, sprinkled with parsley.

York Salad

York salad: ½ exchange per serving
Herb bread: 1¼ exchanges per serving

4 hard-boiled eggs, quartered	175g/6oz cooked York ham, diced
100g/4oz cooked potato, diced	1 large green pepper, sliced
4 tomatoes, peeled and quartered	1 crisp lettuce
8 stoned black olives	vinaigrette dressing (see page 59)

Prepare all the ingredients. Wash and shred the lettuce coarsely. Toss the ingredients in the vinaigrette dressing just before serving. Serve with Herb bread — *1¼ exchanges per serving* (see page 70).

Pancakes with Jam

1½ exchanges per serving   *Cooking time 3 minutes each*

100g/4oz plain flour	2 eggs
pinch salt	2 tablespoons melted butter
200ml/7fl oz milk	diabetic jam (see page 21)
4½ tablespoons water	

Place the flour, salt, milk, water and eggs in a blender and liquidise until smooth. Add the melted butter and liquidise again. Heat a small heavy frying pan and grease with a little butter. When smoking, pour in enough batter to cover the base thinly, tilting the pan to help the batter spread. Return to the heat and cook until the pancake is brown. Turn over with a palette knife and fry a little on the other side. Tip on to a warm plate, spread with a little warmed jam and roll up. Keep warm as the remainder are cooked in the same way. Grease the pan sparingly as necessary. This should make 8-12 pancakes depending on the pan size. Serve with 150ml/¼ pint whipped cream, if liked.

MENU 7

Iced Yogurt and Cucumber Soup

Negligible

300ml/½ pint chicken stock
300ml/½ pint natural yogurt
  (see page 56)
150g/5oz cucumber, grated
  with skin

2 cloves garlic, crushed
juice of ½ lemon
salt

Mix the ingredients in a bowl. Leave in the refrigerator for at least
3 hours before serving.

Celery and Mussel Salad

Celery and mussel salad:
  2 exchanges per serving
Herb bread: ½ exchange
  per serving

Cooking time 30 minutes

450g/1lb potatoes
3 litres/5 pints mussels
4 shallots or 1 small onion
250ml/8fl oz dry white wine
300ml/½ pint mayonnaise
  (see page 57)

1 teaspoon Dijon mustard
inside stalks of 1 head celery
4 hard-boiled eggs, quartered
chopped fresh parsley to garnish

Boil the potatoes and dice. Scrub the mussels and discard any open or broken ones. Place in a large pan with the chopped shallots or onion and wine. Cover tightly and cook for about 5 minutes or until all the mussels are open. Strain the liquid over the diced potatoes. Discard the shells and allow the mussels to cool. Flavour the mayonnaise with the Dijon mustard and mix in the cold mussels, potatoes, sliced celery and hard-boiled eggs. Sprinkle with chopped parsley and serve with Herb bread — ½ *exchange per serving* (see page 70).

Spiced Curd Cheese Tart

2½ exchanges per serving   *Cooking time 30 minutes*
Oven temperature Hot 220°C, 425°F, Gas Mark 7, Moderately Hot
   190°C, 375°F, Gas Mark 5

1 212-g/7½-oz packet frozen
   puff pastry, thawed
225g/8oz curd cheese
1 egg
½ teaspoon mixed spice

grated rind of ½ lemon
25g/1oz currants
150ml/¼ pint double cream,
   whipped (optional)

Roll out the pastry and use to line a 20-30-cm/8-9-inch flan case or sandwich tin. Prick the base with a fork. Combine the cheese, egg, spice and lemon rind. Scatter the currants over the pastry and put the cheese mixture on top. Bake in a hot oven for 10 minutes then reduce the heat to moderately hot for a further 20 minutes or until the filling is set. Serve hot with whipped cream handed separately or cold with the whipped cream spread over the top.

MENU 8

5 exchanges per serving
Serves 2

Chinese Salad

Negligible

½ Chinese cabbage, shredded
1 green pepper, chopped
6 spring onions, chopped
½ cucumber, sliced

2 tablespoons toasted nuts
vinaigrette dressing (see page 59)
1 tablespoon soy sauce

Mix the cabbage, pepper, onions and cucumber. Sprinkle with toasted nuts. Mix 4 tablespoons vinaigrette dressing with the soy sauce in a screw-topped jar. Shake up and dress the salad just before serving.

Cyprus Sausages with Brown Lentils

3¾ exchanges per serving

Cooking time 10 minutes

4 Cyprus sausages (Loukanika)
   or other highly spiced all-meat
   sausage
1 onion, chopped

1 tablespoon olive oil
150g/5oz dry brown lentils,
   cooked

Prick the sausages all over and grill for about 10 minutes, turning once. Fry the onion in the oil until browned. Mix in the cooked lentils. Slice the sausages and arrange on top. Serve with half quantity Cucumber yogurt salad (see page 52).

Hot Coffee Soufflé

1 exchange per serving   *Cooking time about 40 minutes*
Oven temperature Moderately Hot 190°C, 375°F, Gas Mark 5

20g/¾oz butter
20g/¾oz plain flour
150ml/¼ pint milk
2 teaspoons instant coffee powder
 or granules

2 tablespoons water
2 eggs, separated
2 teaspoons Tia Maria or rum

Butter a 1-litre/1½-pint soufflé dish or ovenproof glass dish. Melt the butter in a saucepan, remove from the heat and add the flour. Blend in the milk. Return to the heat and stir until the mixture thickens. Add the coffee dissolved in the water. Beat in the egg yolks and add the liqueur. Whisk the egg whites until soft peaks form. Stir a spoonful of egg white into the coffee mixture then carefully fold in the remainder. Pour into the prepared dish and bake in a moderately hot oven for 20-25 minutes or until well risen. Serve at once with White custard (see page 67).

MENU 9

Stuffed Leeks à la Greque

Cooking time 30 minutes

6 small leeks
600ml/1 pint water
6 tablespoons olive oil
juice of 1 lemon
6 coriander seeds, crushed
6 whole peppercorns
1 bay leaf
parsley stalks

salt
175-225g/6-8oz halibut steak,
  poached and flaked
4 tablespoons mayonnaise
  (see page 57)
To garnish
1 tablespoon capers
chopped fresh parsley

Trim the outside leaves, the dark green ends and the roots from the leeks.
Boil the water, oil, lemon juice, spices, herbs and seasoning for 10
minutes. Simmer the leeks in this liquid for 15-20 minutes, depending
on size. Drain overnight. Place on a serving dish. Slit carefully
lengthwise, leaving the bottom ends joined. Fill the cavities with the
halibut mixed with mayonnaise. Garnish with capers and chopped
parsley.

Turkey Fillets with Mushrooms and Soured Cream

*Potato crisps: 1 exchange
  per serving*

Cooking time 45-50 minutes

2 turkey breast portions
25g/1oz butter
150ml/¼ pint light stock
bouquet garni

salt and pepper
100g/4oz mushrooms, sliced
150ml/¼ pint soured cream

Beat the turkey portions with a rolling pin to flatten them. Melt the butter in a pan and gently cook the turkey breasts for 1 minute on each side, to seal without browning. Pour over the stock, add the bouquet garni and seasoning. Cover and simmer for 30 minutes. Add the sliced mushrooms and cook for a further 10 minutes. Stir in the soured cream and gently reheat to simmering point. Adjust the seasoning. Serve with potato crisps (*1 exchange per serving*) and green beans.

For a 5-exchange menu serve with extra potato crisps – 1 exchange per serving.

Dried Apricot Fool

3 exchanges per serving

Cooking time about 30 minutes

120g/4½oz dried apricots
1 tablespoon apricot brandy

4 tablespoons double cream, whipped

Soak the apricots overnight in 450ml/¾ pint water. Simmer until tender, adding more water if necessary. Cool. Press through a sieve or liquidise in a blender. Add the apricot brandy and fold in the whipped double cream. Make an attractive marbled effect by not mixing too thoroughly. Pour into 2 glasses or sundae dishes.

MENU 10

5 exchanges per serving
Serves 2

Watercress Soup

½ exchange per serving   *Cooking time 30 minutes*

25g/1oz butter
1 bunch watercress, chopped
1 small onion, chopped
1 50-g/2-oz potato, peeled and
  sliced

300ml/½ pint light stock
salt and pepper
6 tablespoons milk

Melt the butter, add the watercress and onion and cook without colouring for about 5 minutes. Add the potato, stock and seasoning. Bring to the boil and simmer for 20 minutes. Allow to cool slightly. Add the milk and liquidise in a blender. Adjust the seasoning and reheat gently. Do not boil.

Nut Roast

3½ exchanges per serving   *Cooking time 55 minutes*
Oven temperature Moderately Hot 200°C, 400°F, Gas Mark 6

225g/8oz onion, chopped
1 tablespoon olive oil
50g/2oz bacon, chopped
1 clove garlic, crushed
225g/8oz mixed nuts, chopped
  (walnuts, hazelnuts and
  almonds — mixture not to
  exceed *1 exchange*)

100g/4oz fresh wholewheat
  breadcrumbs
salt and pepper
1 tablespoon chopped fresh
  parsley
1 egg, beaten

Fry the onion in the oil with the bacon and garlic. Stir in the nuts, breadcrumbs and seasoning. Add the parsley and beaten egg. Mix well and pour into a greased 0.5-kg/1-lb loaf tin and bake in a moderately hot oven for 45 minutes. Serve with half quantity Mixed green salad (see page 49).

Note   This quantity of nut roast is over-generous for two people as the *exchange* value makes half the portion *4½ per serving*. I advise, therefore, making this quantity and cutting off a slice to eat cold later. Nut roast is excellent cold.

Almond Custard

1 exchange per serving   *Cooking time 50 minutes*
Oven temperature Cool 150°C, 300°F, Gas Mark 2

300ml/½ pint milk
2 artificial sweetener tablets
1 egg
1 egg yolk

15g/½oz ground almonds
2 drops almond essence
15g/½oz toasted flaked almonds
  to decorate

Heat the milk with the artificial sweetener. Beat the egg, egg yolk and ground almonds together. Pour on the milk, add the almond essence and pour into a 450ml/¾-pint ovenproof dish. Cover with greaseproof paper or foil. Place in a roasting tin with water to come halfway up the dish. Bake in a cool oven for 50 minutes or until set. Cool and scatter with toasted flaked almonds.

MENU 11

5 exchanges per serving
Serves 4

Mixed Green Salad with Cheese

1 lettuce
selection of: ½ green pepper,
  2 heads chicory, bunch
  watercress, 1 celery heart,
  ½ cucumber

100g/4oz Emmenthal cheese,
  cut in thin strips
25g/1oz grated Parmesan cheese
vinaigrette dressing (see page 59)

Wash the salad and drain well. Toss with the cheeses and vinaigrette
dressing. Serve at once.

Beef Goulash

Beef goulash: 2 exchanges per
  serving
Pan-roasted potatoes:
  2 exchanges per serving
Oven temperature Cool 150°C, 300°F, Gas Mark 2

Cooking time 3–4 hours

1kg/2lb lean stewing beef
75g/3oz flour
1 teaspoon salt
black pepper
3–4 tablespoons oil
4 onions, sliced
4 tomatoes, peeled and chopped

2 bay leaves
8 prunes
1 clove garlic, crushed
2 teaspoons paprika
300ml/½ pint red wine
2 tablespoons natural yogurt

Cut the meat into 5-cm/2-inch squares. Put the flour, salt and pepper into a paper bag, drop in the meat and shake the bag vigorously to coat evenly. Heat the oil and brown the meat, a few pieces at a time, to seal. Transfer to a flameproof casserole. Brown the onions and add to the casserole with the tomatoes, bay leaves, prunes, garlic and paprika. Pour over the wine and bring to the boil on top of the cooker. Cover the casserole tightly with foil and the lid. Place in a cool oven for 3-4 hours or until the meat is tender. Just before serving, stir in the yogurt. Serve with Pan-roasted potatoes — *2 exchanges per serving* (see page 45) and a green vegetable such as broccoli.

Pineapple Ice Cream

1 exchange per serving

1 small pineapple	4 100-g/4-oz portions vanilla
2 tablespoons rum	ice cream

Peel the pineapple, remove the eyes and the hard central core. Cut 175g/6oz of the prepared pineapple into small dice. Pour over the rum and allow to macerate overnight. Mix the fruit and juice into the softened ice cream. Pour into an ice tray and refreeze before serving.

MENU 12

5 exchanges per serving
Serves 4

Smoked Eel with Egg Custard

1 exchange per serving
Oven temperature Moderate 160°C, 325°F, Gas Mark 3

Cooking time 30 minutes

175m/6fl oz double cream
2 eggs, beaten
salt and pepper

4 small thin slices of black bread
225g/8oz smoked eel, thinly sliced
lemon wedges to garnish

Warm the cream and add to the beaten eggs with the seasoning. Beat thoroughly and strain into a shallow baking dish. Place the dish in a baking tin with water to come halfway up the dish. Bake in a moderate oven for about 30 minutes or until the custard is set. Cool. Just before serving, cut in slices and arrange on the slices of black bread. Top with sliced smoked eel and garnish with wedges of lemon.

Nut Loaf

2 exchanges per serving
Oven temperature Moderate 180°C, 350°F, Gas Mark 4

Cooking time about 1½ hours

4 onions, finely chopped
50g/2oz butter
100g/4oz mushrooms, chopped
450g/1lb mashed potato (use
675g/1½lb raw potatoes)

350g/12oz mixed nuts, chopped
(hazelnuts, almonds, Brazil
nuts, walnuts)
salt and pepper

Fry the onions in the butter until transparent. Add the mushrooms and cook for 2 minutes. Mix with the mashed potato and set aside. Prepare the almonds and walnuts by standing them in boiling water for 10-15 minutes and then removing the skins. Place all the nuts on a baking tray and allow to brown in a moderate oven (160°C, 325°F, Gas Mark 3) for about 20 minutes. Rub the skins from the hazelnuts. Chop all the nuts coarsely and add to the potato mixture. Season well. Spoon into a well greased 1-kg/2-lb loaf tin and bake in a moderate oven for about 1 hour. Turn out on to a warmed dish and serve with Mixed green salad (see page 49).

Chocolate Eclairs

2 exchanges per serving   *Cooking time 35-40 minutes*
Oven temperature Moderately Hot 200°C, 400°F, Gas Mark 6

1 quantity choux pastry
  (see page 66)

300ml/½ pint double cream,
  whipped
175g/6oz diabetic chocolate

Make up the choux pastry as instructed. Put the mixture into a piping bag fitted with a 1-cm/½-inch plain nozzle. Pipe the pastry through on to a lightly greased baking tray, making eight 7.5-cm/3-inch lengths. Bake in a moderately hot oven for 35-40 minutes until well risen, golden brown and dry inside. Test by splitting, if steam comes out, return to the oven for a few more minutes. Cool. Split and fill with whipped cream. Melt the chocolate on a plate over a gently steaming pan of water and dip the tops of the eclairs into the chocolate to cover them.

MENU 13

Avocado Dip

Melba toast: 1 exchange per serving

1 ripe avocado
50-100g/2-4oz curd cheese
salt and pepper

2-3 spring onions, chopped
lemon wedges to garnish

Peel the avocado, remove the stone and mash with the curd cheese, using a fork. Add seasoning to taste. Place on individual plates and sprinkle with the chopped spring onions. Garnish with lemon wedges and serve with Melba toast — *1 exchange per serving* (see page 21).

Spareribs of Pork with Sesame Seeds

Potato crisps: 1¾ exchanges
  per serving
Oven temperature Hot 230°C, 450°F, Gas Mark 8

Cooking time 1 hour

12 spareribs of pork
1 tablespoon sesame oil

50g/2oz sesame seeds

Brush the spareribs with oil and place on a rack over a baking tin. Roast in a hot oven for 1 hour. Fry the sesame seeds in a dry frying pan until the seeds pop and turn a light brown. Shake the pan continuously to prevent burning. Serve the spareribs with English mustard, soy sauce and the sesame seeds. Serve with half quantity Mixed green salad (see page 49) and potato crisps (*1½ exchanges per serving*).

For a 5-exchange menu serve with extra potato crisps – 1 exchange.

Baked Apples with Cream Sauce

1½ exchanges per serving   *Cooking time 1½ hours*
Oven temperature Cool 150°C, 300°F, Gas Mark 2

2 225-g/8-oz Bramley apples	1 tablespoon sultanas
25g/1oz walnuts, chopped	rind and juice of 1 orange

Core the apples. With the point of a knife, draw a line round the circumference of each apple, to prevent bursting during cooking. Combine the nuts, sultanas and orange rind. Use this mixture to fill the cavities. Pour the orange juice over the apples and bake in a cool oven for 1½ hours. Serve at once with Cream sauce (see page 64).

MENU 14

Apple and Herring Salad

1 exchange per serving

2-3 rollmop herrings,
   depending on size
2 large dessert apples

1 small onion
150ml/¼ pint soured cream

Cut the herrings into 2.5-cm/1-inch pieces. Core the apples but do not peel and cut into thin slices. Slice the onion into rings. Mix the herring, apple and onion together in a bowl. Divide on to individual plates and spoon over the soured cream.

Pork Chops with Coconut Garnish

Plain boiled rice: 3 exchanges
   per serving

Cooking time about 20 minutes

2 large pork chops
salt and pepper

1 tablespoon olive oil

Trim the chops, rub with salt, pepper and olive oil. Grill for about 10 minutes on each side. Serve with plain boiled rice *(3 exchanges per serving)* and coconut garnish (see opposite).

Coconut Garnish

Negligible   *Cooking time about 15 minutes*

1 tablespoon peanut oil
1 onion, chopped
1 clove garlic, crushed
½ teaspoon ground coriander

½ teaspoon ground cumin
½ teaspoon salt
100g/4oz desiccated
   coconut

Heat the oil and fry the onion and garlic. When soft and just colouring, add the spices and cook for 2 minutes, stirring all the time. Add the coconut and continue frying the mixture, again stirring continually until golden. Drain on kitchen paper. When cold, store in an airtight container.

Custard Cream Pots with Melba Sauce

1 exchange per serving   Cooking time 1-1¼ hours
Oven temperature Cool 150°C, 300°F, Gas Mark 2

piece of vanilla pod
300ml/½ pint milk
1 egg

1 egg yolk
2 artificial sweetener tablets
   (optional)
Melba sauce (see page 63)

Put the vanilla pod in a pan with the milk and bring slowly to the boil. Beat the egg and egg yolk thoroughly. Remove the vanilla pod, add the sweetener and pour the milk on to the egg mixture and blend. Strain into individual ramekins. Stand the ramekins in a baking tin with water to come halfway up the dishes. Cover with foil and bake in a cool oven for 1-1¼ hours. Test by inserting a knife into the custard, it should come out clean when the custard is ready. Serve chilled, topped with Melba sauce.

Note   While the oven is on at this temperature, take the opportunity to make Melba toast (see page 21).

MENU 15

Salmon Pâté

Melba toast: 1¼ exchanges per serving

175g/6oz cooked salmon or turbot
50g/2oz butter
squeeze of lemon juice
1 teaspoon chopped chives

salt and pepper
To garnish
lemon wedges
pinch chopped chives

Flake the fish and mash with a fork. Add the softened butter and beat well. Mix in the lemon juice and chives and season with salt and pepper. Divide between individual dishes and sprinkle with chives. Place a lemon wedge on each serving. Serve with Melba toast — *1¼ exchanges per serving* (see page 21).

Gratin Savoyarde

Gratin Savoyarde:
  2 exchanges per serving
Cole slaw salad:
  ¾ exchange per serving
Oven temperature Hot 230°C, 450°F, Gas Mark 8

Cooking time 30 minutes

1 clove garlic
150ml/¼ pint milk
salt and pepper
225g/8oz potatoes, sliced wafer
  thin

75g/3oz Emmenthal cheese,
  grated
75g/3oz unsalted butter
175g/6oz York ham, cut in 4 slices

Butter a fireproof dish and rub the cut clove of garlic around the inside. Pour in the milk and add the seasoning. Place half the potatoes in the milk, cover with half the cheese and half the butter in dabs. Arrange the other half of the potatoes on top and scatter over the remaining cheese and butter. Cook on top of the cooker for 10 minutes and then in a hot oven for about 20 minutes until the top is golden brown. Serve with thick slices of York ham and Cole slaw salad — ¾ *exchange per serving* (see page 50).

Grapefruit Jelly

1 exchange per serving

Cooking time 5 minutes

4 tablespoons water
7g/¼oz gelatine
250ml/8fl oz fresh grapefruit
  juice

4 artificial sweetener tablets
pinch citric acid
4 tablespoons double cream,
  whipped

Put the water in a small saucepan, scatter over the gelatine and leave to soak for a few minutes. Melt it, without boiling, over a gentle heat. Add the grapefruit juice, artificial sweetener and citric acid. Leave to cool until almost set. This can be speeded up by standing the pan in iced water. On the point of setting, fold in the whipped cream and pour into 2 individual glass dishes.

MENU 16

5 exchanges per serving
Serves 2

Courgette Salad

Cooking time 15 minutes

450g/1lb courgettes
4 tablespoons olive oil
1 onion, finely chopped
2 tablespoons white wine vinegar

1 teaspoon crushed coriander
  seeds
salt and pepper

Slice the unpeeled courgettes very thinly. Heat the oil in a frying pan and gently cook the courgettes and onion over a low heat for 5 minutes, stirring occasionally. Do not allow to brown. Add the vinegar and coriander and continue cooking until the courgettes are just tender. Season and serve at room temperature.

Chicken with Sesame

Chicken with sesame:
  ½ exchange per serving
Pommes Anna:
  1½ exchanges per serving
Oven temperature Hot 220°C, 425°F, Gas Mark 7

Cooking time 40 minutes

2 chicken joints
20g/¾oz breadcrumbs
1 tablespoon sesame seeds

salt and pepper
15g/½oz butter, melted

Dip the dry chicken joints in a mixture of breadcrumbs, sesame seeds and seasoning. Place in a roasting tin, pour over the melted butter and roast in a hot oven for 40 minutes. Serve with Pommes Anna — *1½ exchanges per serving* (see page 48).

Prune Fool

3 exchanges per serving

Cooking time about 5-10 minutes

150g/5oz dry prunes
cold tea to cover
strip of lemon peel
2-4 artificial sweetener tablets

1 tablespoon Kirsch
4 tablespoons double cream,
  whipped

Wash the prunes and soak overnight in the tea. Cook them gently in the same liquid with a strip of lemon peel, adding water if necessary. When the prunes are tender, add the artificial sweetener to taste. Cool. Remove the lemon peel and the stones from the prunes. Liquidise the prunes in a blender with the liqueur. When cold, fold in the whipped cream and serve.

MENU 17

Leeks Vinaigrette

Cooking time about 10 minutes

675g/1½lb small leeks
1 teaspoon chopped fresh thyme

vinaigrette dressing (see page 59)

Remove the green part of the leeks. Split the white part and wash thoroughly. Cook in boiling salted water for about 10 minutes until tender. Drain overnight in a colander. Add the chopped thyme to the vinaigrette dressing and pour over the leeks.

Veal Chops in Soured Cream

Veal chops in soured cream: negligible
Mashed potatoes: 3½ exchanges per serving

Cooking time about 15 minutes

4 large veal chops
1 tablespoon seasoned flour
(see page 64)

50g/2oz butter
150ml/¼ pint soured cream
salt and pepper

Put the chops in a paper bag with the seasoned flour and shake to coat the meat. Melt the butter in a frying pan and fry the chops very gently without browning for 2 minutes on each side. Pour over the cream and simmer for about 10 minutes. Serve with Grilled tomatoes (see page 39) and mashed potatoes (*3½ exchanges per serving*).

For a 5-exchange menu serve with extra mashed potatoes – 1 exchange.

Tipsy Coffee Jelly

15g/½oz gelatine or 1 envelope
600ml/1 pint strong coffee, made
   with 2 tablespoons powdered
   coffee or 4 tablespoons ground
   coffee

2-4 artificial sweetener tablets
2 tablespoons whisky

Soak the gelatine in 3 tablespoons of the cold coffee for 5 minutes. Melt without boiling and add to the remainder of the sweetened coffee. Cool and stir in the whisky. Pour into 4 tall glasses and leave to set. Serve with White custard (see page 67).

MENU 18

4 exchanges per serving
Serves 2

Avgolemono

Cooking time 10 minutes

1 chicken bouillon cube
600ml/1 pint boiling water
2 egg yolks

juice of 1 small lemon
chopped fresh parsley to garnish

Dissolve the bouillon cube in the water. Beat the egg yolks with the lemon juice. Add a little of the hot stock and stir. Pour this egg mixture into the pan of stock and heat without boiling. If boiled, it will curdle. Serve at once, sprinkled with chopped parsley.

Trout with Hazelnuts

Sauté potatoes:
*   2 exchanges per serving*
Oven temperature Moderate 180°C, 350°F, Gas Mark 4

Cooking time 20-30 minutes

50g/2oz hazelnuts
2 trout
salt and pepper

25g/1oz butter
1 grapefruit

Place the nuts in a roasting tin and toast in the oven until the skins flake off and the nuts are brown. Rub the nuts in a rough cloth to remove the skins, then chop roughly. Fill the cavities of the trout with the nuts. Arrange the fish in a greased, shallow ovenproof dish. Season liberally and dot with butter. Bake in a moderate oven for 10 minutes.

Using a sharp serrated knife, cut the skin and pith from the grapefruit. Cut into segments. Scatter over the fish and continue cooking for 10-20 minutes, depending on the size of the trout. Serve with Sauté potatoes — *2 exchanges per serving* (see page 46).

For a 5-exchange menu serve with extra sauté potatoes — 1 exchange.

Fried Bananas in Brandy

2 exchanges per serving   *Cooking time about 8 minutes*

3 100-g/4-oz bananas   1 tablespoon brandy
50g/2oz butter   2 tablespoons soured cream

Peel the bananas. Melt the butter in a frying pan and, when foaming, add the bananas. Fry gently for about 5 minutes until brown and soft. Just before serving, pour over the brandy. Remove the bananas to serving plates and allow the butter and brandy to slightly thicken in the pan before pouring over the fruit. Serve immediately with a spoonful of soured cream.

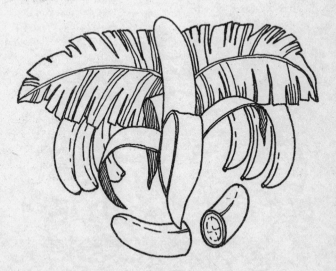

MENU 19

5 exchanges per serving
Serves 2

Carrot Soup

Carrot soup:
  ½ exchange per serving
Croûtons: ½ exchange per serving

Cooking time about 30 minutes

40g/1½oz butter
2 onions, chopped
1 teaspoon curry paste
225g/8oz carrots, grated
600ml/1 pint stock or water

salt and pepper
1 tablespoon chopped fresh
  parsley
2 tablespoons single cream

Melt the butter, add the onions and cook without colouring for about 5 minutes. Add the curry paste and cook for a further 2 minutes. Add the carrots, stock and seasoning. Bring to the boil and simmer for 15 minutes. Press through a sieve or liquidise in a blender. Add the chopped parsley. Stir in the cream at the last minute and serve with toasted cubes of bread (croûtons) — *½ exchange per serving.*

Pizza

2 exchanges per serving   *Cooking time 20 minutes*
Oven temperature Moderately Hot 200°C, 400°F, Gas Mark 6

100g/4oz frozen puff pastry,
  thawed
1 tablespoon tomato purée
75g/3oz Emmenthal cheese,
  grated
4 black olives, stoned and
  quartered

4 green olives, stoned and
  quartered
4 anchovy fillets
pinch marjoram
1 teaspoon olive oil

Roll out the pastry and line two 10-cm/4-inch individual tins. Prick
the bases a few times with a fork. Brush the tomato purée on to the
pastry and scatter over the cheese. Arrange the olives and anchovies on
top. Sprinkle with marjoram and olive oil and bake in a moderately hot
oven for 20 minutes. Serve with half quantity Mixed green salad (see
page 49).

Fried Apples with Ice Cream

2 exchanges per serving   *Cooking time about 8 minutes*

2 100-g/4-oz Bramley apples
25g/1oz butter

2 100-g/4-oz portions Cornish
  dairy ice cream
2 tablespoons Calvados

Peel and core the apples. Slice into 4 rings. Melt the butter in a frying
pan and carefully fry the apple rings without breaking them. Place the
ice cream in 2 serving dishes, arrange 2 apple rings on each and pour
over the Calvados. Serve immediately.

MENU 20

Red Bean Soup

1 exchange per serving

Cooking time about 50 minutes using a pressure cooker

2 onions, chopped
3 carrots, diced
5 sticks celery, sliced
2 cloves garlic, crushed
1 tablespoon beef dripping
75g/3oz red beans, soaked overnight
2 tablespoons tomato purée

1 tablespoon salt
1.75 litres/3 pints water or stock (see page 61)
fresh parsley
1 225-g/8-oz packet frozen spinach (optional)
2 tablespoons dry sherry

Soften the onions, carrots, celery and garlic in the beef dripping for about 4 minutes. Add the beans, tomato purée, salt and stock or water. Pressure cook for 35 minutes. Remove about 300ml/½ pint soup, cool slightly and place in a blender. Add a handful of parsley (take care not to include any stalks), liquidise until smooth and return to the pan. Add the frozen spinach and sherry. Heat gently until the spinach has melted. Serve with natural yogurt, if liked.

Turkish Meat Pasties

2 exchanges per serving   *Cooking time 30 minutes*
Oven temperature Moderately Hot 190°C, 375°F, Gas Mark 5

½ quantity shortcrust pastry
  (see page 65)
Filling
2 tablespoons oil
1 onion, chopped
225g/8oz minced beef
1 clove garlic, crushed

4 tablespoons sultanas
2 tablespoons chopped fresh
  parsley
salt and pepper
1 egg or 1 egg yolk and 1
  tablespoon water to glaze

To make the filling, heat the oil and fry the onion until soft. Add the minced beef and garlic and stir until browned. Remove from the heat, add the sultanas, parsley and seasoning and leave to cool. Make the pastry and roll out thinly. Cut into eight 10-cm/4-inch circles. Divide the meat mixture between them, damp the edges with water, fold over and seal. Brush with beaten egg, place on a baking sheet and bake in a moderately hot oven for 20 minutes. Serve with Mixed green salad (see page 49).

Danish Cheeseboard

Oatcakes: 2 exchanges per serving

The Danes have been making cheeses since the days of the Vikings and their products are justifiably enjoyed all over the world. Their popularity makes them easily obtainable almost everywhere.
Danablu is the most famous of all Danish cheeses with its distinctive flavour and piquant aroma. It is almost white in colour with dark blue veins. This is a soft textured cheese which spreads easily. *Danbo* is made with caraway seeds. Aromatic *Esrom* is delicate and butterlike with numerous irregular holes. *Havarti* is fuller flavoured, piquant with a strong aroma. *Samsoe* is a deliciously light mild cheese. Try serving Danish cheese with sliced green pepper rings, sticks of celery, pieces of fennel and Oatcakes — *2 exchanges per serving* (see page 69).

MENU 21

4 exchanges per serving
Serves 2

Poor Man's Caviar

Melba toast: 2 exchanges per serving   *Cooking time 40 minutes*
Oven temperature Moderately Hot 190°C, 375°F, Gas Mark 5

1 large aubergine
4 tablespoon olive oil
salt and pepper

1 large clove garlic, crushed
2 tablespoons chopped fresh
parsley

Bake the aubergine in a moderately hot oven for about 40 minutes.
When the aubergine is quite soft, and cool enough to handle, remove the
skin and mash the pulp roughly. Add the olive oil, drop by drop, stirring
continuously, so that it is gradually completely absorbed. Season with
salt, pepper and garlic. Sprinkle with parsley and serve with lemon
wedges and Melba toast — *2 exchanges per serving* (see page 21).

Grilled Plaice

Duchesse potatoes:
2 exchanges per serving

Cooking time about 10 minutes

2 225-g/8-oz plaice, on the bone
salt and pepper

25g/1oz butter

Cut three slits on either side of the fish and season with salt and pepper. Grease the grill grid with some of the butter, melt the rest and brush over the fish. Cook for approximately 5 minutes on each side. Serve with Grilled tomatoes (see page 39), Tartare sauce (see page 58) and Duchesse potatoes — *2 exchanges per serving* (see page 45).

For a 5-exchange menu serve with extra Duchesse potatoes – 1 exchange.

Mocha Mousse

Negligible

35g/1¼oz diabetic chocolate
1 tablespoon strong black coffee
1 tablespoon rum

1 egg
2 tablespoons soured cream

Break up the chocolate. Put in a bowl over a pan of steaming water, add the coffee and rum and allow to melt. Separate the egg and beat the yolk into the chocolate mixture. Whisk the egg white until it forms soft peaks and fold in. Pour into 2 ramekin dishes. Leave overnight in a cool place. Just before serving, top with soured cream.

MENU 22

5 exchanges per serving
Serves 2

Chicken Consommé

Negligible

Cooking time 5 minutes

1 440-g/15½-oz can jellied
  chicken consommé
1 tablespoon dry sherry
juice of ½ lemon
sprig of fresh tarragon

To garnish
2 tablespoons soured cream
pinch chopped fresh tarragon
  leaves

Heat the consommé gently. Add the sherry, lemon juice and sprig of tarragon. Leave to cool and then chill. Before serving remove the tarragon, which will have imparted its flavour. Mix the soured cream with the pinch of tarragon leaves. Serve the consommé in individual bowls with a spoonful of the flavoured soured cream on top.

Frankfurters and Potato Salad

3 exchanges per serving

Cooking time 20 minutes

350g/12oz new potatoes
150ml/¼ pint mayonnaise
  (see page 57)
4 frankfurter sausages

To garnish
1 tablespoon chopped fresh
  parsley
1 tablespoon chopped gherkin

Scrub but do not peel the potatoes and cook in boiling salted water until tender. Skin and toss with mayonnaise while still warm. Cool and chill. Slice the frankfurters into 2.5-cm/1-inch pieces and add to the potato salad. Serve garnished with parsley and gherkin.

Plum Fool

2 exchanges per serving   *Cooking time about 20 minutes*

350g/12oz plums
2–4 artificial sweetener tablets

150ml/¼ pint double cream, whipped
1 tablespoon Kirsch

Wash the plums. Cut in half and remove the stones. Stew the fruit in the minimum of water required to prevent burning. When soft, press the fruit through a sieve or liquidise in a blender with the artificial sweetener. Allow to cool completely before folding in the whipped cream and Kirsch.

MENU 23

5 exchanges per serving
Serves 2

Ratatouille

Melba toast: 1 exchange per serving   *Cooking time 30 minutes*

4 tablespoons olive oil
1 large onion, sliced
1 red or green pepper, halved,
  deseeded and sliced
1 large aubergine, unpeeled and
  diced

1 clove garlic, crushed
2 tomatoes, peeled
salt and pepper
chopped fresh parsley

Heat the oil in a heavy pan and add the onion. Cover with the lid and cook for a few minutes until soft. Add the pepper, aubergine and garlic and cook for a further 10 minutes. Add the tomatoes. Cover and simmer until the vegetables have absorbed the oil. Add seasoning to taste. Chill. Sprinkle with parsley and serve with Melba toast — *1 exchange per serving* (see page 21).

Lamb Chops with Bacon

3 exchanges per serving   *Cooking time about 20 minutes*

2 lamb chops
oil
salt and pepper

4 rashers of bacon
175g/6oz egg noodles
25g/1oz butter

Brush the chops with a little oil. Sprinkle with salt and pepper and place under a preheated grill. Cook for about 5 minutes on each side, depending on thickness. Remove the rind from the bacon and add to the grill when turning the chops over. Meanwhile, cook the noodles in plenty of boiling salted water for 10 minutes or as instructed on the packet. Drain well. Melt the butter in the pan and return the drained noodles. Shake over a gentle heat. Add the seasoning. Turn the noodles on to a warmed serving dish, arrange the chops and bacon on top and pour over the pan juices.

Lime Soda

1 exchange per serving

3 tablespoons fresh lime juice   soda water
2 100-g/4-oz portions Cornish
   dairy ice cream

Put the lime juice into 2 tall glasses and add a scoop of ice cream to each. Fill with soda water to taste. Serve at once with drinking straws and long handled spoons.

MENU 24

4 exchanges per serving
Serves 2

Artichoke Vinaigrette

Cooking time 30-40 minutes

2 globe artichokes
salt

vinaigrette dressing (see page 59)

Wash the artichokes under running cold water pulling back the leaves to rinse thoroughly. Place in a large pan of boiling salted water and simmer for 30-40 minutes, depending on size. Test by pulling off the leaves at the base of the choke. They should come away easily. Drain well, upside down. Cool. Gently pull back the leaves from the centre to reveal the choke, carefully pull it out and discard. Chill.

To eat a globe artichoke, pull off each leaf and dip the base into individual bowls of vinaigrette dressing. Eat the fleshy part of the leaf. The base (heart) of the artichoke is the best part.

Sautéed Kidneys with Pourgouri

Sautéed kidneys:
  1½ exchanges per serving
Pourgouri: 2 exchanges per serving

Cooking time 55 minutes

50g/2oz butter
4 sheeps' kidneys, skinned, halved
  and cored
175g/6oz chipolata sausages
2 onions, chopped
100g/4oz mushrooms, quartered
  if large

25g/1oz flour
1 teaspoon tomato purée
150ml/¼ pint stock
1 tablespoon dry sherry
1 bay leaf
salt and pepper
chopped fresh parsley to garnish

Melt the butter in a frying pan and brown the kidneys and sausages. Remove to a heated plate. Put the onions in the pan and cook until soft. Add the mushrooms and cook for a further 5 minutes. Sprinkle over the flour and add the tomato purée. Stir until the flour is browned. Add the stock, sherry, bay leaf and seasoning. Bring to the boil, replace the kidneys and sausages and simmer for 30 minutes. Adjust the seasoning. Pour into a warmed serving dish and scatter with chopped parsley. Serve with Pourgouri — *2 exchanges per serving* (see page 44).

For a 5-exchange menu serve with extra pourgouri – 1 exchange.

Junket

½ exchange per serving   *Cooking time 5 minutes*

150ml/¼ pint single cream   artificial sweetener to taste
150ml/¼ pint milk   1 teaspoon rennet
1 tablespoon dry sherry   nutmeg, grated

Bring the cream and milk to blood heat. Add the sherry and remove from the heat. Add the artificial sweetener and rennet. Pour the mixture into 2 individual pots. Cover and allow to set, but do not refrigerate. Grate the nutmeg on top.

Note 300ml/½ pint milk may be substituted for the mixed milk and cream.

MENU 25

5 exchanges per serving
Serves 2

Tomato Soup

1 exchange per serving   *Cooking time 30 minutes*

350g/12oz tomatoes, peeled and   salt and pepper
  chopped   150ml/¼ pint water
1 onion, chopped   ½ chicken bouillon cube
25g/1oz slice crustless bread   2 tablespoons double cream
300ml/½ pint milk

Put the tomatoes and onion in a pan and cook gently for 15 minutes. Add the bread, milk, seasoning, water and bouillon cube. Bring to the boil and simmer for 15 minutes. Place in a blender and liquidise or press through a sieve. Reheat gently. Add a swirl of cream to each serving.

Note The success of this soup depends upon using fresh and not canned tomatoes.

Cheese Tart

4 exchanges per serving   *Cooking time 40 minutes*
Oven temperature Moderately Hot 190°C, 375°F, Gas Mark 5

175g/6oz shortcrust pastry   1 tablespoon chopped fresh
  (see page 65)   parsley
25g/1oz butter   175g/6oz Cheddar cheese, grated
1 bunch of spring onions, chopped   salt and pepper
4 eggs

Make the pastry and use to line a 23-cm/9-inch flan tin or dish. Bake the pastry blind in a moderately hot oven for 15 minutes. Melt the butter and fry the spring onions until soft but not browned. Scatter the onions over the pastry. Beat the eggs with the parsley and add the cheese and seasoning, making sure you do not use too much salt if the cheese is salty. Pour the mixture into the pastry case and bake for a further 25 minutes. Serve with Tomato, onion and pepper salad (see page 51).

Coffee Jelly

Negligible   *Cooking time 10 minutes*

½ tablespoon instant coffee powder or granules
1-2 artificial sweetener tablets
150ml/¼ pint water

1 teaspoon gelatine
75ml/2½fl oz milk
2 size 6/small eggs, separated
2 drops vanilla essence

Dissolve the coffee powder and artificial sweetener in a little hot water taken from the 150ml/¼ pint. Allow to cool and add the gelatine. Leave to soak. Bring the remaining water and milk to the boil. Add the beaten egg yolks to a little cooled milk and water. Blend and strain back into the pan. Stir over a gentle heat until the mixture just coats the back of a spoon. Do not boil. Stir in the coffee and gelatine mixture and add the vanilla essence. Cool and chill over iced water. When almost set, whisk the egg whites until stiff and fold into the jelly mixture. Pour into a bowl to set.

MENU 26

5 exchanges per serving
Serves 2

Jellied Salad

1 exchange per serving

Cooking time 10 minutes

175g/6oz fresh pineapple,
   chopped
300ml/½ pint water
2 teaspoons gelatine

1 avocado
50g/2oz curd cheese
juice of ½ lime

Place the pineapple in 150ml/¼ pint of the water, bring to the boil and cool. Add the gelatine to the remaining 150ml/¼ pint water and leave to stand for 5 minutes. Dissolve over a gentle heat and set aside to cool. Peel and slice the avocado and arrange in a glass dish or mould. When the gelatine mixture is almost cold, add the curd cheese, lime juice and drained pineapple. Spoon carefully over the avocado and leave to set. Serve on a bed of lettuce leaves.

Curried Eggs with Savoury Rice

4 exchanges per serving

Cooking time 50 minutes

4 hard-boiled eggs
Sauce
2 tablespoons oil
1 onion, finely chopped
¼ teaspoon each ground ginger,
   chilli, coriander, mace,
   cinnamon, saffron, salt and
   pepper, or 1½ teaspoons mild
   curry powder
2 tablespoons flour
600ml/1 pint water or light stock

150ml/¼ pint natural yogurt
squeeze of lemon juice
Savoury rice
1 tablespoon oil
2 tablespoons chopped spring
   onion
75g/3oz long grain rice, cooked
25g/1oz pine nuts, toasted
squeeze of lemon juice
salt and pepper

To make the sauce, heat the oil and gently cook the chopped onion until light brown. Add the spices or curry powder and cook for a few minutes. Add the flour and blend in the water or stock. Bring to the boil, stirring continuously. Simmer for about 40 minutes, stirring frequently, until reduced by about half.

Just before serving, add the yogurt and lemon juice. Pour over the freshly boiled eggs and serve with savoury rice. To prepare the rice, heat the oil and fry the spring onion gently. Add the cooked rice, pine nuts, lemon juice and seasoning and heat through.

Chocolate Orange Mousse

Negligible

Cooking time about 5-8 minutes

45g/1¾oz diabetic (plain)
   chocolate
8g/¼oz butter, softened
1 egg yolk
1 tablespoon orange juice

zest of ½ orange
½ tablespoon Cointreau
1 egg white, stiffly beaten
soured cream (optional)

Melt the chocolate in a bowl over boiling water. Add the softened butter and beat in the egg yolk. Add the orange juice, zest and liqueur. Place the mixture into the refrigerator. When thoroughly cold, fold in the stiffly beaten egg white. Pour the mousse mixture into 2 individual pots and leave in a cool place. Do not refrigerate. Serve with a spoonful of soured cream if liked.

MENU 27

5 exchanges per serving
Serves 2

Chicken Liver Pâté

Melba toast: 1¼ exchanges
per serving

Cooking time about 6 minutes

25g/1oz butter
225g/8oz chicken livers, trimmed
½ clove garlic, crushed
1 tablespoon brandy

salt and pepper
150ml/¼ pint double cream,
 whipped

Melt the butter and fry the livers with the garlic until brown outside but still pink inside. Place in a blender. Pour the brandy into the frying pan, heat and stir until the pan is clean. Pour this over the livers, add the seasoning and liquidise until smooth. When cold, fold in the whipped cream. Pour into an earthenware serving dish and refrigerate overnight. Serve with Melba toast — *1¼ exchanges per serving* (see page 21).

Ham and Chicory Bake

Ham and chicory bake:
 ¾ exchange per serving
Jacket potatoes:
 3 exchanges per serving
Oven temperature Moderately hot 200°C, 400°F, Gas Mark 6

Cooking time about 35 minutes

4 heads chicory
4 slices ham
butter

½ quantity White sauce
 (see page 55)
25g/1oz Cheddar cheese, grated

Cook the heads of chicory in boiling salted water until tender. Drain well, preferably overnight. Wrap each head of chicory in a slice of ham and arrange in a shallow buttered ovenproof dish. Coat with white sauce and sprinkle with grated cheese. Bake in a moderately hot oven for about 25 minutes. Serve with Jacket potatoes — *3 exchanges per serving* (see page 46).

Grilled Grapefruit

Negligible   *Cooking time 10 minutes*

2 grapefruit   15g/½oz butter
4 tablespoons sherry

Halve the grapefruit and loosen the segments with a grapefruit knife or small sharp knife. Pour a tablespoon of sherry over each of the 4 halves. Dot with butter and grill for 10 minutes or until the fruit is hot.

ENTERTAINING MENUS

MENU 1

Taramasalata

Taramasalata: ¾ exchange per serving
Melba toast: 1½ exchanges per serving

3 25-g/1-oz slices crustless white
  bread
3–4 tablespoons milk
100g/4oz smoked cod's roe,
  fresh or bottled
2 cloves garlic, crushed

175ml/6fl oz olive oil
pepper
To garnish
chopped fresh parsley
black olives
lemon wedges

Soak the bread in the milk for 5 minutes. Squeeze dry and put in a mixing bowl. Add the cod's roe and garlic. Add the oil drop by drop, stirring continuously. Add a little pepper; it should not need salt. Garnish with chopped parsley, black olives and lemon wedges. Serve with Melba toast — *1½ exchanges per serving* (see page 21).

Kebabs with Pourgouri

Pourgouri: 2 exchanges per serving *Cooking time 10 minutes*

1 small leg of lamb
6 tablespoons olive oil
1½ tablespoons lemon juice
1 teaspoon marjoram

salt and pepper
1 bunch of spring onions or
  100g/4oz shallots

Cut the lamb into 5-cm/2-inch cubes. Mix together the oil, lemon juice, marjoram and seasoning. Add the lamb and marinate overnight. Thread the lamb cubes on to skewers with a piece of spring onion or shallot after every third piece of meat. Grill for 10 minutes, turning as the meat browns. Serve with Tomato, onion and pepper salad (see page 51) and Pourgouri — *2 exchanges per serving* (see page 44).

Strawberry Fool

¾ exchange per serving

450g/1lb strawberries, hulled
1 tablespoon Grand Marnier or
  Cointreau

300ml/½ pint double cream,
  whipped

Mash the strawberries and add the liqueur. Fold in the whipped cream, pour into a bowl and chill before serving.

MENU 2

5 exchanges per serving
Serves 4

Cheesy Choux Balls

2 exchanges per serving   *Cooking time 30-40 minutes*
Oven temperature Moderately Hot 200°C, 400°F, Gas Mark 6

1 quantity choux pastry
  (see page 66)
salt and pepper
cayenne pepper
40g/1½oz butter
40g/1½oz plain flour

300ml/½ pint milk, infused with
  a bouquet garni (see page 177)
100g/4oz strong Cheddar cheese,
  grated
salt and pepper
1 bunch of watercress to garnish

Make up the choux pastry and add the seasoning. Pipe or spoon 12 small balls on to a greased baking sheet. Bake in a moderately hot oven for 30-40 minutes until golden brown and completely dried out.

Meanwhile, melt the butter in a pan. Add the flour, off the heat and blend in the infused milk. Return to the heat and bring to the boil, stirring all the time. Boil for 1 minute, adding a little more milk if it becomes too thick. Remove from the heat and stir in the cheese and seasoning to taste. Split the cooked choux pastry balls in half, spoon in the cheese sauce and replace the tops. Serve immediately on a bed of watercress.

Coq au Vin

Coq au vin: negligible
Pan-roasted potatoes:
  2 exchanges per serving

Cooking time about 1 hour and
  20 minutes

50g/2oz butter
4 chicken joints
100g/4oz gammon rasher, cut in
  strips
100g/4oz button onions or
  100g/4oz onion, sliced
1 clove garlic, crushed

300ml/½ pint red wine or
  150ml/¼ pint red wine and
  150ml/¼ pint chicken stock
bouquet garni (see page 177)
salt and pepper
15g/½oz butter, softened
15g/½oz plain flour
chopped fresh parsley to garnish

Melt the butter in a fireproof casserole or thick saucepan with a lid and
brown the chicken joints. Remove from the pan. Add the gammon strips
and button onions and fry gently for a few minutes. Add the garlic, red
wine, stock if used, bouquet garni, seasoning and chicken joints. Bring
to the boil, cover and simmer for about 1 hour or until the chicken is
tender. Remove from the heat. Mix the butter and flour together and
add in small pieces to the pan. Stir carefully into the liquid and return to
the heat. Bring back to the boil to thicken the sauce. Adjust the seasoning
and garnish with parsley. Serve with Braised celery (see page 38),
sautéed mushrooms, and Pan-roasted potatoes — *2 exchanges per
serving* (see page 45).

Ice Cream with Hot Chocolate Sauce

1 exchange per serving

Cooking time 8-10 minutes

225g/8oz Cornish dairy ice cream
Sauce
150g/5oz plain diabetic chocolate

9 tablespoons milk
25g/1oz butter

Cut the chocolate into small pieces and put into a small pan with the
milk. Stir over a gentle heat until the chocolate has melted. Add the
butter. Simmer gently until the mixture coats the back of the spoon.
Divide the ice cream between 4 serving dishes, pour over the sauce and
serve immediately.

MENU 3

Gazpacho

Negligible

1396-g/14-oz can tomatoes
1 clove garlic, crushed
1 tablespoon olive oil
1 tablespoon wine vinegar or
  lemon juice
150ml/¼ pint water
salt and pepper

50g/2oz black olives, chopped
50g/2oz cucumber, unpeeled
  and diced
50g/2oz green pepper, chopped
6 spring onions, chopped
1 hard-boiled egg, chopped
  (optional)

Liquidise the tomatoes with the garlic, oil, vinegar, water and seasoning. Pour into a large bowl. Add the remaining ingredients, stir and chill before serving.

Roast Stuffed Guinea Fowl

Roast stuffed guinea fowl: *Cooking time 1¼ hours*
  1½ exchanges per serving
Mashed potatoes:
  1 exchange per serving
Oven temperature Hot 220°C, 425°F, Gas Mark 7, Moderately Hot
  200 °C, 400°F, Gas Mark 6

2 guinea fowl
225g/8oz fat bacon
2 tablespoons plain flour
salt and pepper
Stuffing
100g/4oz sausagemeat
2 teaspoons brandy
2 teaspoons port
2 teaspoons chopped fresh
  parsley

50g/2oz fresh breadcrumbs
salt and pepper
1 clove garlic, crushed
Gravy
6 tablespoons port, red wine or
  sherry
6 tablespoons water
2 bunches of watercress to garnish

To make the stuffing, mix all the ingredients together. Stuff the birds and cover the breasts with fat bacon. Place in a baking tin and roast in a hot oven for 15 minutes. Reduce the heat to moderately hot and continue roasting for a further 45 minutes. Remove the bacon and sprinkle the birds with flour sifted with salt and pepper. Return to the oven and continue cooking for another 15 minutes. Cut each guinea fowl in half and keep warm. Place the roasting tin over the heat and pour in a mixture of port, red wine or sherry and water. Boil and stir until the liquid is of a syrupy consistency to serve as gravy. Arrange the halves of guinea fowl on a bed of watercress and serve with mashed potatoes (*1 exchange per serving*) and gravy.

★ *For a 5-exchange menu serve with extra mashed potatoes – 1 exchange per serving.*

German Cheeseboard

Oatcakes: 1½ exchanges per serving

There is a wide variety of German cheeses from which to choose. Among the hard cheeses, I recommend German *Emmenthal*. It has a dark yellow to brown rind, covering a pale yellow inside. The holes in this cheese should be evenly distributed, as round as possible and as large as cherries. Try *Bergkäse*, *Tilsit* and *Biarom* with caraway, too. Among the soft cheeses, *Limburg* is particularly delicious. It has a spicy aroma. All German cheeses go particularly well with wine and Oatcakes — 1½ *exchanges per serving* (see page 69).

MENU 4

5 exchanges per serving
Serves 4

Chilled Mushroom Casserole

Herb bread: ¾ exchange per serving   *Cooking time about 15 minutes*

1 tablespoon oil
15g/½ oz butter
1 onion, sliced
450g/1lb mushrooms, sliced
5-cm/2-inch piece of fresh ginger
   root, grated

150ml/¼ pint water
2 tablespoons tomato purée
2 tablespoons dry sherry
1 tablespoon soy sauce
salt and pepper

Heat the oil and butter in a pan, add the onion and mushrooms, and sauté for a few minutes. Add the ginger, water, tomato purée, sherry, and soy sauce. Simmer for 10 minutes. Adjust the seasoning and chill. Serve in individual dishes with Herb bread — *¾ exchange per serving* (see page 70).

Roast Duck with Apple Sauce

Roast potatoes:
  2¼ exchanges per serving
Apple sauce:
  1 exchange per serving
Oven temperature Moderately Hot 200°C, 400°F, Gas Mark 6

Cooking time 1½ hours

1 1.5-kg/3½-lb duck
salt and pepper
675g/1½lb potatoes, halved

50g/2oz butter, melted
1 bunch of watercress to garnish

Dry the duck thoroughly inside and out. Rub the skin with salt and prick all over with a fork. Place breast side down on a rack over a roasting tin and cook on the lower shelf of a moderately hot oven for 30 minutes. Turn over, prick all over again and return to the oven for 1 hour.

Meanwhile, parboil the potatoes for 5 minutes, drain and transfer to a roasting tin. Pour over the butter, sprinkle with salt and pepper and roast on the top shelf for 1 hour. Serve the duck and potatoes on a bed of watercress. Hand Apple sauce — *1 exchange per serving* — separately (see page 63).

Melon Cheese Salad

1 exchange per serving

800g/1¾lb melon, diced
8 Petit Suisse cheeses

8 tablespoons double cream, whipped
2 tablespoons toasted almonds

Place half the melon into bowls. Beat the cheese until smooth and fold in the whipped cream. Stir the remaining melon into this mixture and spoon into the bowls. Top with almonds.

MENU 5

4 exchanges per serving
Serves 2

Egg Mousse

Cooking time 15 minutes

3 eggs
175ml/6fl oz double cream,
  whipped

2 teaspoons anchovy essence
½ teaspoon Worcestershire sauce
salt and pepper

Lower the eggs into a pan of fast boiling water and boil for 15 minutes. Remove and plunge into cold water. When quite cold, peel, cut in half and remove the yolks. Chop the whites and add to the whipped cream, with the anchovy essence and Worcestershire sauce. Sieve the the yolks and add to the mixture. Season and spoon into ramekins. Chill before serving.

Trout with Almonds

Trout with almonds:
  1 exchange per serving
Garlic bread:
  1 exchange per serving

Cooking time about 20 minutes

50g/2oz shredded almonds
50g/2oz butter
2 trout
25g/1oz seasoned flour
  (see page 64)

juice of ½ lemon
1 tablespoon chopped fresh
  parsley

Fry the almonds in half the butter until golden brown. Drain on kitchen paper and keep hot. Melt the rest of the butter in the frying pan. Dip the trout into the seasoned flour and place in the foaming butter. Lower the heat and cook the fish for 5 minutes on each side. Remove to a warmed serving dish and sprinkle with the almonds. Add the lemon juice and parsley to the butter in the pan and heat. Pour over the trout. Serve with Garlic bread — *1 exchange per serving* (see page 70).

*For a 5-exchange menu serve with extra garlic bread – 1 exchange per serving.

Peach Melba

2 exchanges per serving

2 100-g/4-oz fresh peaches
juice of ½ lemon

2 heaped tablespoons Cornish dairy ice cream
Melba sauce (see page 63)

Skin the peaches, cut in half and remove the stones. Dip in lemon juice to prevent discolouration. Fill each peach half cavity with ice cream and spoon over Melba sauce. Serve immediately.

MENU 6

Avocado Soup

Negligible

2 ripe avocados
1 teaspoon curry paste
600ml/1 pint chicken stock
(bouillon cubes may be used)

150ml/¼ pint double cream
juice of ½ lemon
salt and pepper

Remove the skin and stones from the avocados. Place in a blender with the curry paste, warmed chicken stock, cream, lemon juice and seasoning. Liquidise until smooth. Chill. Adjust the seasoning before serving.

Spiced Lamb with Pourgouri

Pourgouri: 3 exchanges per serving   Cooking time about 2 hours
Oven temperature Hot 220°C, 425°F, Gas Mark 7, Moderate 160°C, 325°F, Gas Mark 3

2 cloves garlic, crushed
1 onion
20g/¾oz fresh ginger, sliced
¼ teaspoon ground cumin or
coriander
2 cloves

pinch chilli powder
juice of ½ lemon
½ teaspoon salt
25g/1oz ground almonds
2 tablespoons natural yogurt
1 shoulder of lamb

Place the garlic, onion, spices, lemon juice, salt, almonds and yogurt in a blender and liquidise to a paste. Spread over the lamb. Roast in a hot oven for 15 minutes, turning the lamb over to seal after 7 minutes. Reduce the oven heat to moderate and cook for about 1½ hours or until tender. Prepare the pourgouri (see page 44). Serve the spiced lamb and pourgouri — *3 exchanges per serving* — with Mushroom and broad bean salad (see page 53).

★For a 5-exchange menu serve with extra pourgouri – 1 exchange.

Oranges in Grand Marnier

1 exchange per serving

4 large oranges   2 tablespoons Grand Marnier

Using a sharp serrated knife, cut the skin and pith from the oranges. Cut in thin slices and arrange in a serving dish. Spoon over the liqueur and leave to soak for a few hours, covered, in the refrigerator.

MENU 7

5 exchanges per serving
Serves 4

Celeriac Salad

Celeriac salad: Negligible
Melba toast: ½ exchange per serving

1 450-675-g/1-1½-lb head
  celeriac
150-300-ml/¼-½ pint
  mayonnaise (see page 57)

Dijon mustard
salt and pepper

Wash and peel the celeriac. Cut into matchstick pieces and mix with mayonnaise flavoured with the mustard and seasoning. Serve on lettuce leaves with Melba toast — *½ exchange per serving* (see page 21).

Javanese Saté

Plain boiled rice:
  4 exchanges per serving

Cooking time 5 minutes
  (rice about 20 minutes)

450-675g/1-1½lb rump steak,
  cut into 1-cm/½-inch cubes
Marinade
2 tablespoons soy sauce
6 tablespoons lemon juice

1 clove garlic, crushed
1 tablespoon ground cumin
To serve
225g/8oz cooked long grain rice
coconut garnish (see page 99)

Mix the ingredients for the marinade and add the cubes of steak. Cover and leave overnight. Thread the steak on to skewers and cook under a hot grill for 5 minutes, turning frequently. Arrange the skewers on a bed of hot plain boiled rice and hand the coconut garnish separately.

Yogurt and Hazelnut Whip

½ exchange per serving   *Cooking time 5 minutes*

50g/2oz shelled hazelnuts   150ml/¼ pint double cream,
350ml/12fl oz home-made   whipped
  yogurt (see page 56)

Brown the hazelnuts in a hot oven or very carefully in the grill pan under the grill. Cool and rub off the skins with your fingers. Chop roughly. Fold the yogurt and whipped cream lightly together, and add most of the hazelnuts. Divide between 4 glasses and scatter over the remaining hazelnuts.

MENU 8

4 exchanges per serving
Serves 2

Crudités

½ small cauliflower
100g/4oz young carrots
100g/4oz young turnips
1 bunch spring onions
1 celery heart
4 small sweet tomatoes

Dressing
1 clove garlic, crushed
1 teaspoon chopped fresh mint
  or basil
150ml/¼ pint mayonnaise
  (see page 57)

Cut the cauliflower into small florets. Cut the carrots and turnips into strips. Wash and trim the spring onions. Slice the celery heart into 2 pieces. Arrange the raw vegetables on a serving plate. Stir the garlic and mint or basil into the mayonnaise. Spoon this dressing into individual dishes for each person to dip into with the raw vegetables.

Tournedos

Pan-roasted potatoes:
  3½ exchanges per serving

Cooking time 12-15 minutes

1 tablespoon olive oil
15g/½oz butter
2 tournedos steaks,
  4cm/1½ inches thick

4 tablespoons dry sherry
150ml/¼ pint rich stock
  (see page 61)
salt and pepper

Heat the oil and butter in a frying pan. When hot, put in the tournedos, seal for 1 minute on each side over a high heat. Reduce the heat and cook gently for 3½ minutes on each side for rare, or 4½ minutes on each side for medium. Remove the steaks to a warmed dish. Turn up the heat and pour in the sherry, stir to dissolve the meat sediment. Add the stock and boil until the mixture is syrupy. Add seasoning, if necessary, and then pour the sauce over the steaks. Serve with Pan-roasted potatoes — *3½ exchanges per serving* (see page 45) and French beans.

For a 5-exchange menu serve with extra pan-roasted potatoes – 1 exchange.

Yogurt Whip

½ exchange per serving

5 tablespoons double cream
200ml/7fl oz natural yogurt
  (see page 56)

grated nutmeg

Whip the cream lightly and stir the yogurt until smooth. Fold the yogurt into the cream and divide between 2 glasses. Dust a little freshly grated nutmeg on each.

MENU 9

Green Pea Soup

½ exchange per serving

450g/1lb frozen peas
1 lettuce heart, shredded
1 teaspoon salt

Cooking time about 10 minutes

600-900ml/1-1½ pints light
  chicken stock
50g/2oz butter
chopped fresh chervil

Put the peas, shredded lettuce, salt and enough of the stock to barely cover. Simmer for 5 minutes. Liquidise with the remaining stock. Return to the pan and bring almost to the boil. Adjust the seasoning, stir in the butter and, when melted, sprinkle with chopped chervil.

Veal Chops with Grapes

Veal chops with grapes:
  1 exchange per serving
Duchesse potatoes:
  2 exchanges per serving

Cooking time about 30 minutes

50g/2oz butter
4 veal chops
6 tablespoons dry vermouth
salt and pepper

4 tablespoons double cream
225g/8oz white grapes, peeled,
  halved and seeded

Melt the butter in a pan with a lid. Add the chops and brown for about 2 minutes on each side. Pour over the vermouth and season with salt and pepper. Simmer, covered, for 15-20 minutes depending on the thickness of the chops. Just before serving, add the cream and grapes. Reheat gently and adjust the seasoning, if necessary. Serve with Duchesse potatoes — *2 exchanges per serving* (see page 45).

*For a 5-exchange menu serve with extra Duchesse potatoes – 1 exchange.

Café Liégeoise

½ exchange per serving

600ml/1 pint cold strong black coffee

4 100-g/4-oz portions Cornish dairy ice cream

6 tablespoons double cream, whipped

Fill 4 tumblers three quarters full with the cold coffee. Float a scoopful of ice cream on each and top with whipped cream. Assemble just before serving. Use long handled spoons and drinking straws.

MENU 10

5 exchanges per serving
Serves 2

Beansprout and Watercress Soup

Cooking time 10 minutes

450ml/¾ pint chicken stock
½ bunch watercress, chopped
100g/4oz bean sprouts

½ teaspoon lemon juice
salt and pepper

Bring the stock to the boil. Add the chopped watercress and simmer for 3 minutes. Stir in the beansprouts and simmer for a further 2 minutes. Add the lemon juice and seasoning to taste.

Pork with Almonds

Plain boiled rice:
  4 exchanges per serving

Cooking time about 20 minutes

50g/2oz whole almonds,
  blanched
2 tablespoons oil
1 small onion, finely chopped
225g/8oz pork tenderloin,
  cut into 2.5-cm/1-inch cubes
¼ cucumber, peeled and
  thickly sliced

150ml/¼ pint chicken stock
1 teaspoon cornflour
1 tablespoon sherry
salt and pepper
100g/4oz long grain rice, boiled,
  to serve

First dry fry the almonds until light brown. Keep hot. Heat the oil and fry the onion for 1 minute. Add the pork and cucumber and continue frying fairly briskly for another 2 minutes. Mix the stock and cornflour together and pour into the pan. Add the sherry and seasoning and stir until the liquid thickens. Finally, add the almonds and serve at once with plain boiled rice — *4 exchanges per serving.*

Hot Vanilla Soufflé

1 exchange per serving   Cooking time 25 minutes
Oven temperature Moderately Hot 190°C, 375°F, Gas Mark 5

25g/1oz butter
200ml/7fl oz milk
piece of vanilla pod

20g/¾oz plain flour
2 eggs, separated
artificial sweetener to taste

Grease 2 individual soufflé dishes with a little of the butter. Heat the milk with the vanilla pod and bring slowly to just below boiling point. Allow to cool for 5 minutes to thoroughly infuse the flavour. Meanwhile, melt the remaining butter in a pan, add the flour, off the heat, and strain on the milk. Stir well to blend, return to the heat and bring slowly to the boil, stirring all the time. Allow to cool a little, then beat in the egg yolks, one at a time. Add the artificial sweetener to taste. (At this stage, the process can be halted if preparations are being made in advance.) Whisk the egg whites until they form soft peaks and carefully fold into the vanilla mixture. Divide between the 2 dishes. Place in a moderately hot oven and bake for 15 minutes or until well risen.

MENU 11

Iced Vichyssoise

½ exchange per serving · *Cooking time about 30 minutes*

225g/8oz leeks, white part only, chopped
50g/2oz onion, chopped
50g/2oz butter
100g/4oz potatoes, sliced

600ml/1 pint water or light chicken stock
salt and pepper
175ml/6fl oz double cream
2 tablespoons chopped fresh chives

Sweat the leeks and onion in the butter without browning. Add the potatoes. Pour over the boiling water or stock and add 1 teaspoon salt. Simmer for 20 minutes. Allow to cool slightly. Pour into the blender and liquidise until smooth. Cool. Add the cream and chives and chill thoroughly. Adjust seasoning before serving.

Salmon with Almond or Walnut Sauce

New potatoes:
    2 exchanges per serving   *Cooking time 1-1½ hours*
Oven temperature Moderate 180°C, 350°F, Gas Mark 4

1.5kg/3lb salmon or salmon trout
50g/2oz butter, melted
salt and pepper
Sauce
50g/2oz almonds or walnuts

150ml/¼ pint double cream, lightly whipped
2 tablespoons freshly grated horseradish (not horseradish cream)
juice of ½ lemon

Brush the surface of the fish with the butter. Season well. Wrap the fish in a loose parcel of foil and bake in a moderate oven for 1-1½ hours.

Meanwhile, make the sauce. Pour boiling water over the nuts to remove their skins. Chop. Stir lightly into the cream and add the horseradish. Season and add the lemon juice. Serve the salmon with the sauce, tiny new potatoes (*2 exchanges per serving*) and cucumber salad.

Gâteau Paris Brest

2½ exchanges per serving   *Cooking time 35 minutes*
Oven temperature Hot 230°C, 450°F, Gas Mark 8

1 quantity choux pastry
  (see page 66)
150ml/¼ pint milk
25g/1oz flaked almonds
Filling
225g/8oz dessert apples,
  peeled and grated

2 tablespoons water
leafy sprig of sweet cicely
300ml/½ pint double cream,
  whipped

Make up the choux pastry as directed but substitute milk for water. Pipe a large circle of pastry on to a greased baking tray and sprinkle the top with the flaked almonds. Bake in a hot oven for about 35 minutes. Split carefully to make sure that the choux ring is dried out inside. Return to the oven to dry further, if necessary. Cool on a wire rack.

Meanwhile, cook the grated apple in the water with the sweet cicely. When soft, remove the herb and cool. When cold, fold into the whipped cream. Fill the split choux ring with the apple cream just before serving.

MENU 12

5 exchanges per serving
Serves 4

Mushroom Soup

¾ exchange per serving   *Cooking time 25-30 minutes*

50g/2oz butter
350g/12oz large flat mushrooms, chopped
1 clove garlic, crushed
900ml/1½ pints light chicken stock or water and a bouillon cube

salt and pepper
50g/2oz slice of crustless white bread
1 tablespoon chopped fresh parsley

Melt the butter, add the mushrooms and garlic. Cook, stirring, until the butter has been absorbed. Add the stock, seasoning and the slice of bread, torn in pieces. Simmer for 15 minutes. Allow to cool slightly. Liquidise in a blender. Adjust the seasoning, add the chopped parsley and hand soured cream separately, if liked.

Roast Fillet of Beef

Pan-roasted potatoes: *Cooking time 45 minutes*
   3½ exchanges per serving
Oven temperature Hot 220°C, 425°F, Gas Mark 7

1.25kg/2½lb fillet of beef   15g/½oz butter, melted

Trim the fillet and tie neatly with string. Place on a rack in a roasting tin and brush with melted butter. Roast in a hot oven for 45 minutes. Stand in a warm place for 10 minutes. This will make it easy to carve. Serve with Garlic butter (see page 62), Leaf spinach (see page 41) and Pan-roasted potatoes — *3½ exchanges per serving* (see page 45).

Raspberry Fool

¾ exchange per serving

450g/1lb raspberries   300ml/½ pint double cream

Wash the raspberries in a sieve and drain well. Liquidise in a blender then press through a sieve to remove the seeds. Whip the cream until it just holds its shape and fold in the raspberry purée. Chill thoroughly before serving.

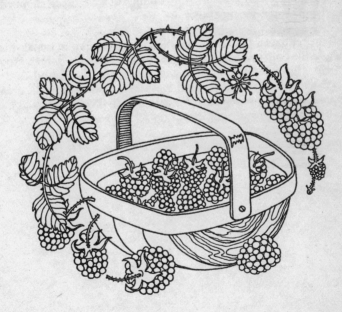

MENU 13

4 exchanges per serving
Serves 4

Ham and Watercress Mousse

Ham and watercress mousse:
  ¼ exchange per serving
Crispbread:
  1¼ exchanges per serving

Cooking time 10 minutes

15g/½oz butter
15g/½oz plain flour
150ml/¼ pint beef stock
150ml/¼ pint tomato juice
1½ teaspoons (½ envelope)
  gelatine
1 teaspoon Worcestershire sauce

1 tablespoon sherry
salt and pepper
150ml/¼ pint double cream,
  whipped
100g/4oz cooked ham, chopped
1 bunch of watercress, chopped

Melt the butter, add the flour and blend in the stock and tomato juice. Bring to the boil, stirring all the time. Soak the gelatine in 1 tablespoon water for a few minutes, add to the sauce and stir until dissolved. Add the Worcestershire sauce, sherry and seasoning. Cool. Stir in the cream, chopped ham and watercress. Pour into individual dishes and chill. Serve with crispbread — *1¼ exchanges per serving*.

*For a 5-exchange menu serve with extra crispbread – 1 exchange.

Grilled Sole with Fennel in Cream Sauce

Fennel in cream sauce:
½ exchange per serving

Cooking time 10 minutes

4 small sole
50g/2oz butter, melted

salt and white pepper

Cut three diagonal slashes on each side of the sole. Place on the greased rack of a grill pan. Brush with melted butter and season with salt and white pepper. Grill for 5 minutes. Turn over, brush with butter and season. Grill for a further 5 minutes. Serve with Fennel in cream sauce — *½ exchange per serving* (see page 41).

Italian Cheeseboard

Oatcakes: 2 exchanges per serving

The Italians produce many more cheeses than we are familiar with. Most cooks use ready grated *Parmesan* in pasta dishes and soups, but few know how superb this cheese is fresh. Among highly recommended varieties to try are *Gorgonzola* from the Po valley, *Mozzarella*, which was once made from buffalo milk but is now produced from cow's milk with excellent results, *Provolone*, butterlike *Italico* and aromatic *Taleggio*. Serve with Oatcakes — *2 exchanges per serving* (see page 69).

MENU 14

Cold Almond Soup

¾ exchange per serving

100g/4oz unblanched almonds
600ml/1 pint cold water
2 tablespoons olive oil
2 cloves garlic, crushed

¼ teaspoon salt
juice of ½ lemon
50g/2oz seedless white grapes

Pour boiling water over the almonds. Leave for 3 minutes, then remove the skins. Place in a blender with the water, oil, garlic and salt. Liquidise until smooth. Chill. Add the lemon juice and adjust the seasoning. Peel the grapes and divide between the 2 bowls of soup.

Veal Escalopes with Marsala

Veal escalopes with Marsala:
  ½ exchange per serving
New potatoes:
  2¾ exchanges per serving

Cooking time 15 minutes

2 veal escalopes
squeeze of lemon juice
1 tablespoon seasoned flour
25g/1oz butter

2 tablespoons Marsala
salt and pepper
2 tablespoons double cream
little stock

Sprinkle the veal escalopes with lemon juice. Dip them in the seasoned flour and fry quickly in the butter until brown on both sides. Add the Marsala and allow it to bubble for a few minutes. Add the seasoning and cream. Stir well to take up the meat juices from the base of the pan. Add a little stock if the sauce becomes too thick. Serve with new potatoes (2¾ *exchanges per serving*) and pickled cucumber.

Pears in Wine

1 exchange per serving   *Cooking time 5-10 minutes*

2 ripe pears
150ml/¼ pint rosé or red wine
2.5-cm/1-inch piece of
   cinnamon stick

strip of orange peel
3 tablespoons double cream,
   whipped (optional)

Peel the pears, halve and scoop out the core using a teaspoon. Heat the wine in a pan, with a base just large enough to fit in the 4 pear halves. Add the cinnamon stick and orange peel, and simmer for 5-10 minutes depending on ripeness of the pears. Remove the cinnamon and orange peel. Serve hot in individual bowls with a spoonful of whipped cream added just before serving.

MENU 15

Jellied Soup

Cooking time 5 minutes

1 396-g/14-oz can consommé
1 tablespoon dry sherry

1 85-g/3-oz packet cream cheese
1 50-g/2-oz jar lumpfish roe

Warm the consommé in a pan with the sherry and cream cheese until the ingredients are well blended. Allow to cool. Divide the roe between 4 soup bowls. Pour the soup over carefully and chill in the refrigerator.

Grilled Sea Bass

Potato crisps:
  2 exchanges per serving

Cooking time about 30 minutes

1 1-kg/2-lb sea bass
100g/4oz butter
2 teaspoons ground fennel seeds

2 tablespoons Pernod
salt and pepper
lemon slices to garnish

Ask the fishmonger to clean the fish. Make diagonal slits in the flesh and stuff with a mixture of the butter and ground fennel seeds. Use half for each side of the fish. Place the fish on the greased rack of a grill pan. Spoon over 1 tablespoon Pernod. Grill under a medium heat for about 15 minutes. Turn over. Pour over the remaining Pernod and grill for a further 15 minutes. Garnish with lemon slices. Serve with lettuce and watercress dressed with a sharp dressing, and potato crisps — *2 exchanges per serving*.

Stilton and Oatcakes

Oatcakes: 2 exchanges per serving

Stilton is considered to be the monarch of English cheeses. It is made from whole milk with added cream and takes a long time to ripen. It should be bought whole and served scooped from the centre with a spoon. A little dry sherry or port should be poured into the cavity and left to soak into the cheese. Serve with Oatcakes — *2 exchanges per serving* — (see page 69) and butter.

For a 5-exchange menu serve with extra oatcakes – 1 exchange.

MENU 16

Crab and Avocado Mould

100g/4oz frozen crabmeat,
   chopped
1 avocado, peeled and diced
6 spring onions, chopped
2 sticks of celery, chopped
2 teaspoons chopped tarragon

salt and pepper
1 envelope gelatine
1½ tablespoons water
200ml/7fl oz tomato juice
1 teaspoon Worcestershire sauce
watercress to garnish

Mix the crabmeat, avocado, onions, celery, tarragon and seasoning together. Soak the gelatine in the water, melt and add to the tomato juice and Worcestershire sauce. Stir in the crab and vegetable mixture and pour into a dampened 600-ml/1-pint mould or soufflé dish. Chill. Turn out on to a serving plate and garnish with sprigs of watercress.

Roast Beef and Yorkshire Pudding

Roast beef and Yorkshire pudding: *Cooking time about 1 hour*
   2 exchanges per serving
Roast potatoes:
   2 exchanges per serving
Oven temperature Moderately Hot 200°C, 400°F, Gas Mark 6,
   Hot 220°C, 425°F, Gas Mark 7

50g/2oz dripping or lard
1-1.25kg/2-2¼lb joint of beef
Gravy
1 teaspoon flour
300ml/½ pint beef stock
3 tablespoons red wine
salt and pepper

100g/4oz plain flour
50g/2oz dripping or lard
Yorkshire pudding
200ml/7fl oz milk
4½ tablespoons water
pinch salt
1 egg

Heat the dripping in a roasting tin in a moderately hot oven. Put in the joint and baste with the hot fat. Calculate 15 minutes per 450g/1lb and 15 minutes over, allowing longer if you prefer it less rare.

Meanwhile, make the Yorkshire pudding batter. Use a whisk to blend the milk, water, salt, egg and flour or liquidise in a blender. Ten minutes before the beef is cooked, raise the oven temperature to hot and place the joint on the lower shelf of the oven. Spoon the dripping into a patty tray and place on the top shelf to heat. When smoking, pour in the batter and bake for 15-20 minutes until well risen and golden. Take the joint out, place on a serving dish and keep warm (use the bottom of the oven if you have nowhere else). It will be easier to carve if it has stood for a while before serving.

To make the gravy, drain most of the fat from the roasting tin. Add the flour to the meat juices, mix thoroughly, add the stock and red wine and bring to the boil. Adjust the seasoning. Serve the roast beef with the Yorkshire puddings, roast potatoes — *2 exchanges per serving* — and a green vegetable such as Cabbage with caraway seed (see page 38).

Apple Nut Yogurt

1¼ exchanges per serving   *Cooking time 8-10 minutes*

450g/1lb Bramley apples
leafy sprig of sweet cicely
  (optional)

2 tablespoons water
150ml/¼ pint natural yogurt
50g/2oz walnuts, chopped

Wash the apples but do not peel or core. Chop into small pieces. Place in a strong pan with the cicely, if used, and water. Cover tightly and cook gently until the apple is soft. Press through a sieve or vegetable mill. The core, skin and pips will be left behind. Cool. Put the apple purée into a bowl or individual dishes and spoon over the yogurt. Scatter with the chopped walnuts.

MENU 17

5 exchanges per serving
Serves 2

Stracciatelle

1½ exchanges per serving   *Cooking time about 3-5 minutes*

1 egg   600ml/1 pint chicken stock
1 tablespoon semolina   salt and pepper
2 tablespoons grated Parmesan   chopped fresh parsley to garnish
  cheese

Beat the egg with the semolina and cheese. Heat the stock and add a little
to the egg mixture. Whisk this mixture into the pan of hot stock and beat
until the egg curdles. Check the seasoning and scatter in the chopped
parsley.

Stuffed Steak

Sauté potatoes: *Cooking time 12-18 minutes*
  3½ exchanges per serving

2 175-g/6-oz rump steaks,   grated rind of ½ orange
  2.5-cm/1-inch thick   ½ teaspoon chopped mixed
25g/1oz butter   dried herbs
1 small onion, finely chopped   salt and pepper
100g/4oz mushrooms   1 tablespoon melted butter

Using a sharp pointed knife, cut a pocket in each steak, starting with a slit
along the longest side. Melt the butter and fry the onion until soft. Set
aside 2-4 mushrooms, depending on their size, and chop the rest. Add to
the onion and fry for 1 minute. Add the orange rind, herbs and
seasoning. Spoon this mixture into the 2 steak pockets. Secure with
skewers. Brush with melted butter and grill for 3-6 minutes on each side,
depending on preference for rare or well done steak. Grill the whole
mushrooms and arrange on top of the steaks. Serve with Sauté potatoes
— *3½ exchanges per serving* (see page 46) — and a Mixed green salad
(see page 49).

Brown Bread Custard

1 exchange per serving   *Cooking time 20 minutes*
Oven temperature Cool 150°C, 300°F, Gas Mark 2

20g/¾oz fresh brown
  breadcrumbs
1 egg, separated
200ml/⅓ pint milk
2 artificial sweetener tablets

2 teaspoons gelatine
1 tablespoon water
3 drops vanilla essence
150ml/¼ pint double cream,
  whipped

Bake the breadcrumbs until crisp in a cool oven. Cool. Meanwhile, beat
the egg yolk, scald the milk and pour on to the yolk. Mix well, add the
artificial sweetener, return to the pan and stir without boiling until the
mixture thickens. Soak the gelatine in the water until thoroughly
dissolved. Add to the hot custard and stir until the ingredients have
combined. Cool. Flavour with vanilla essence. On the point of setting,
fold in the breadcrumbs, cream and stiffly whisked egg white. Pour into
individual ramekins to set.

MENU 18

4 exchanges per serving
Serves 4

Baked Eggs with Ham

Cooking time 15 minutes
Oven temperature Moderately hot 190°C, 375°F, Gas Mark 5

25g/1oz butter
50g/2oz cooked ham, chopped
150ml/¼ pint single cream

4 eggs
salt and pepper

Grease 4 ramekin dishes with half the butter. Divide the ham between these and spoon over half the cream. Place the dishes in a roasting tin half full of boiling water. Place on top of the cooker and heat until the cream is hot. Break an egg into each dish. Spoon over the remaining cream, dot with the remaining butter and sprinkle with salt and pepper. Bake in the centre of a moderately hot oven for 10 minutes. Serve immediately.

Fish Mayonnaise with Garlic Bread

Garlic bread:
  3 exchanges per serving

Cooking time about 20 minutes

675g/1½lb Scotch salmon or
  turbot, in one piece
25g/1oz butter
salt and pepper
300ml/½ pint mayonnaise
  (see page 57)
1 tablespoon chopped capers

1 tablespoon chopped fresh herbs,
  including chives and parsley
grated rind of 1 lemon
1 lettuce
1 bunch watercress
4 tomatoes
½ cucumber, sliced
lemon wedges to garnish

Dry the fish, smear with butter and sprinkle with salt and pepper. Wrap in greaseproof paper and then a piece of foil or use a boil-in-the-bag. Lower the package into a pan of water. Bring to the boil and simmer gently for 20 minutes. Leave the package of fish to cool in the water. Remove when cold and flake the fish into a large bowl.

Mix the mayonnaise with the capers, herbs and lemon rind. Add to the fish and combine gently but thoroughly. Arrange the salad on a large flat dish. Spoon the fish mayonnaise into the lettuce leaves and garnish with lemon wedges. Serve with Garlic bread — *3 exchanges per serving* (see page 70).

For a 5-exchange menu serve with extra garlic bread — 1 exchange.

Peaches Sour

1 exchange per serving

4 ripe peaches	150ml/¼ pint soured cream
1 tablespoon brandy	50g/2oz flaked almonds, toasted

Peel and slice the peaches and macerate in the brandy for 2 hours, turning occasionally. Fold in the soured cream and spoon the mixture into 4 wine glasses. Top with toasted flaked almonds.

163

MENU 19

Tomato Ice with Prawns

225g/8oz tomatoes, peeled
1 teaspoon lemon juice
2 tablespoons double cream
1 tablespoon tomato ketchup
salt and pepper

1 tablespoon olive oil
2 teaspoons lemon juice
salt and pepper
600ml/1 pint prawns, peeled

Place the tomatoes, lemon juice, cream, tomato ketchup and seasoning in a blender and liquidise. Pour into an ice tray and freeze. Mix the oil and lemon juice with the seasoning. Add the prawns. To serve, cut the tomato ice in slices and spoon the prawns on top. Serve at once.

Chicken Liver Kebabs with Pilaff

Chicken liver kebabs with pilaff:
   3¼ exchanges per serving
Broad bean salad:
   1 exchange per serving

Cooking time about 30 minutes

225g/8oz chicken livers
100g/4oz button mushrooms
4 rashers streaky bacon,
   cut in halves
50g/2oz butter, melted

Pilaff
90g/3½oz long-grain rice
40g/1½oz butter
1 small onion
250ml/8fl oz stock or water
salt and pepper

To prepare the pilaff, wash the rice in a sieve. Melt 15g/½oz butter in a pan. When the butter is foaming, add the rice and stir until the butter thoroughly coats the grains of rice. Liquidise the onion with the stock and add to the rice. Season and simmer, uncovered, for 15-20 minutes. Move the rice occasionally with a fork to prevent sticking.

Thread the livers, with a mushroom or piece of bacon between each piece, on to the skewers. Pour over the melted butter and cook under a hot grill for 8-10 minutes, turning frequently. Do not overcook; the livers should be pink inside. Add the remaining 25g/1oz butter to the pilaff and turn on to a warmed serving dish. Arrange the skewers of liver on top and pour over the juices from the grill pan. Serve with Broad bean salad — *1 exchange per serving* (see page 51).

Raspberry Cream

¾ exchange per serving

150ml/¼ pint double cream
4 tablespoons single cream

1 tablespoon Cointreau or
   ½ teaspoon orange flavouring
225g/8oz raspberries

Whip the creams together until they just hold their shape. Fold in the Cointreau and raspberries. Pile into a small bowl. Cover and chill before serving.

MENU 20

Cream of Peanut Soup

1¼ exchanges per serving   *Cooking time about 20 minutes*

2 onions, chopped
generous 1 litre/2 pints chicken
  stock
225g/8oz salted peanuts

600ml/1 pint milk
4 egg yolks
4 tablespoons dry sherry

Put the onion and 600ml/1 pint of the chicken stock in a pan and cook until the onion is soft. Put in a blender with the peanuts and milk and liquidise. Return to the pan with the remaining stock and bring slowly to the boil. Beat the egg yolks thoroughly and add a little of the hot soup to the yolks. Return this mixture to the pan and heat very gently until the soup thickens. Do not allow to boil. Finally, add the sherry.

Roast Pheasant

Potato crisps: *Cooking time about 1 hour*
  2¼ exchanges per serving
Oven temperature Moderate 180°C, 350°F, Gas Mark 4

25g/1oz butter, softened
1 pheasant
salt and pepper
150ml/¼ pint stock or vegetable
  water

1 tablespoon chopped fresh
  parsley to garnish
Bread sauce to serve
  (see page 58)

Rub the butter over the pheasant. Sprinkle with salt and pepper. Roast in a moderate oven for 1 hour, basting frequently. Remove the bird from the roasting tin, carve and keep hot. Add the stock or vegetable water to the roasting tin and boil until a syrupy consistency is obtained. Pour into a sauce boat. Garnish with parsley and serve with Bread sauce (see page 58), cauliflower or Braised celery (see page 38) and potato crisps — *2¼ exchanges per serving*.

★For a 5-exchange menu serve with extra potato crisps — 1 exchange.

Apple Cream

½ exchange per serving   *Cooking time 8 minutes*

2 225-g/8-oz Bramley apples   200ml/⅓ pint double cream,
2 tablespoons water   whipped
leafy sprig of sweet cicely
   (optional)

Peel, core and slice the apples. Put in a saucepan with the water and cicely, if used, cover and cook to a pulp. Remove the cicely and cool. Fold in the cream. Serve chilled in glasses.

MENU 21

Avocado and Grapefruit Salad

2 grapefruit
1 avocado

vinaigrette dressing
(see page 59)
chopped fresh mint leaves

Using a sharp serrated knife, remove the skin and pith from the grapefruit. Cut each section free of membrane. Peel the avocado and slice with a stainless steel knife. Combine the fruits with the vinaigrette dressing, sprinkle with mint and serve at once.

Guinea Fowl with Almond Sauce

Potato crisps:
  2 exchanges per serving

Cooking time 1 hour

1 guinea fowl
40g/1½oz butter
salt and pepper
pinch fresh or dried marjoram
4 slices streaky bacon

1 clove garlic, crushed
25g/1oz blanched almonds,
  shredded
1 tablespoon sherry
6 tablespoons single cream

Rub the guinea fowl with 25g/1oz of the butter. Sprinkle with salt, pepper and marjoram. Wrap the bacon slices around the bird and secure with string or skewers. Melt the remaining butter in a heavy flameproof casserole. When foaming, put in the bird, breast side down. Lower the heat and cook for 20 minutes. Turn over to the other breast and cook for a further 20 minutes, basting frequently with the juices in the pan. Turn finally on to the back and cook for a final 20 minutes.

Remove from the heat and remove the bacon. Carve the bird and keep hot. Add the garlic and almonds to the juices and cook gently until the almonds are brown. Add the sherry and cream. Simmer very gently for a few minutes then spoon the sauce over the carved meat. Serve with watercress and potato crisps — *2 exchanges per serving.*

★For a 5-exchange menu serve with extra potato crisps — 1 exchange.

English Cheese Board

Oatcakes: 2 exchanges per serving

The manufacture of local English cheeses has resulted in a far greater variety of cheese being readily available. However, some of the more unusual soft and goat cheeses are still only to be found in health food shops. I would strongly advise readers to experiment with English cheeses as they are excellent. Among the more popular are: Cheddar, Stilton, Cheshire, Lancashire, Double and Single Gloucester, which is particularly suitable for toasting. These cheeses are all to be found on the shelves of local supermarkets. Eat with home-made Oatcakes — *2 exchanges per serving* (see page 69).

MENU 22

5 exchanges per serving
Serves 4

Prawn Puffs

2 exchanges per serving   *Cooking time 10-15 minutes*
Oven temperature Hot 220°C, 425°F, Gas Mark 7

225g/8oz peeled prawns
4 tablespoons soy sauce
1 tablespoon dry sherry
pinch ginger

1 212-g/7½-oz packet frozen
  puff pastry
beaten egg to glaze
watercress to garnish

Marinate the prawns in the soy sauce, sherry and ginger for at least 4 hours. Roll out the pastry very thinly and cut into 20 rounds, using a 6-7.5-cm/2½-3-inch cutter. Divide the prawns between these. Wet the edges of the pastry circles and fold over the prawns to form crescents. Seal well and brush with beaten egg. Bake in a hot oven for 10-15 minutes or until well risen and golden brown. Serve hot garnished with sprigs of watercress.

Veal with Potato Pancakes

Veal: ½ exchange per serving   *Cooking time 1½-2 hours*
Potato pancakes:
  1½ exchanges per serving
Oven temperature Moderate 180°C, 350°F, Gas Mark 4

1 (1-kg/2-lb) breast of veal
50g/2oz butter
Stuffing
1 tablespoon oil
1 onion, chopped
50g/2oz mushrooms, chopped

225g/8oz sausagemeat
225g/8oz frozen spinach,
  thawed
1 egg, beaten
juice of ½ lemon
salt and pepper

Bone the veal or ask the butcher to do this for you. Heat the oil and fry the onion until soft, add the mushrooms and cook for 1 minute. Add the onion and mushrooms to the sausagemeat with the chopped spinach, beaten egg, lemon juice and seasoning. Spread this mixture over the veal. Roll up and tie firmly and neatly with string. Melt the butter in a roasting tin, add the veal and baste. Roast in a moderate oven, basting frequently, for 1½-2 hours, depending on size. Protect the veal with foil if it seems dry. Cool and refrigerate overnight. Serve cold in slices with Potato pancakes — *1½ exchanges per serving* (see page 34) — pickled cucumber and Red cabbage salad (see page 33).

Avocado Cooler

1 exchange per serving

1 avocado
175ml/6fl oz fresh orange juice
300ml/½ pint milk

300ml/½ pint single cream
2 bars Cornish dairy ice cream
diabetic chocolate, grated

Remove the flesh from the avocado. Liquidise in a blender with the orange juice. Gradually add the milk and cream. Chill thoroughly. Divide the mixture between 4 tall glasses. Top each glass with half a bar of ice cream and decorate with grated chocolate.

MENU 23

Fondue Bourguignonne

An informal party dish where the meat is cooked by the guests themselves. You will need a special fondue set which is usually made of copper or stainless steel and has its own spirit lamp to keep the oil hot. The meat is cooked by dipping the pieces, one at a time, into the hot oil on a long fork which comes with the set. The meat is then dipped into a sauce from a selection arranged around the fondue and eaten with a variety of garnishes. Serve with a Mixed green salad (see page 49) and French bread. Large bowls of fresh fruit would make a suitable end to the meal.

French bread: 3-4 exchanges
Dessert: 1 exchange

675g/1½lb frying steak, cut into 2.5-cm/1-inch cubes
oil for frying
selection of sauces
mixed green salad (see page 49)
French bread

Garnishes
black and green olives
gherkins
capers
tomatoes, peeled and cut in quarters
spring onions

Prepare the sauces and garnishes and place in small bowls. Arrange these around the fondue set. Place the meat cubes on a plate for each person with an individual salad. When guests are ready to eat, heat the oil in a pan on the cooker. It should be hot but not smoking. Transfer carefully to the fondue pan where it will be kept hot by the spirit burner.

FONDUE SAUCES

Mix the ingredients for each of the sauces together.

Tomato Sauce

150ml/¼ pint mayonnaise
2 tablespoons tomato purée

1 teaspoon Worcestershire sauce

Garlic and Herb Sauce

150ml/¼ pint mayonnaise
1 clove garlic, crushed

1 tablespoon chopped fresh herbs

Mustard Sauce

150ml/¼ pint mayonnaise

2-3 teaspoons Dijon mustard

Curry Sauce

150ml/¼ pint mayonnaise

2-3 teaspoons curry paste

Horseradish Sauce

150ml/¼ pint double cream,
  whipped

2-4 tablespoons horseradish
  sauce, depending on strength

Note It is likely that *3-4 exchanges* will be consumed in the French bread that accompanies the fondue, which is a necessary accompaniment to a rich meal. This will leave just *1 exchange* for the final course. I suggest that the large bowl of fruit contains a small Charentais melon. The diabetic diner will be able to round off his or her meal with 200g/7oz of this highly scented fruit — a suitably fragrant finale to a very special meal.

HERBS AND SPICES

The judicious use of herbs and spices is an essential part of good cooking. It is particularly useful in restricted diets where the provision of one herb or spice over another can transform, say, milk from being the basis of bread sauce – with the addition of clove and bay leaf – to the basis of baked custard – with the addition of a geranium leaf. Chicken can be orientalized with coriander and cumin in a yogurt marinade, or bring back memories of holidays in Normandy by the use of chopped tarragon in a cream sauce. Where sugar is not permitted in a diet, elder flowers or sweet cicely may be added to milk and fruit dishes to provide natural, scented sweetness.

Fresh herbs are nicer than dried. However, their season is a short one and dried herbs are essential during the winter months. For those lucky enough to have a garden, herbs are easy to grow and dry. There is an extensive and helpful literature on the subject – all of which may be borrowed from the public library. For those with only a window sill, French tarragon, chives, parsley, thyme and marjoram – the essentials – will grow on an exterior sill, and basil on the inside.

Spices should always be bought whole (not ground), and loose in small quantities. Not only is this a cheaper way of buying than in expensive packs, but ground spices lose their flavour quickly. I use a coffee grinder in which to grind what I need as I need it. I particularly like the combination of equal quantities of coriander and cumin for use with fried potatoes, and in yogurt for sauces for chicken.

Spices and their Uses

ALLSPICE   Use in soused herrings, pickled vegetables, liver pâté, pot roast, green pea soup, poached fish and spiced lamb.

ANISEED   Use sparingly in soups, stews, salads, cooked vegetables, meat pies and pickles.

CARDOMON SEED   Use ground in curries, stews, pilau. Good with baked apples, in salad dressing and barbecue sauce, with lentil dishes and in coffee.

CARAWAY SEED   Excellent with cabbage, cooked and raw, and in cream cheese. Indispensable in Hungarian goulash.

CAYENNE Use a pinch with oysters, in cheese straws, with fish pâté and in crab and lobster dishes.

CELERY SEED Use in vegetable dishes, soups, stews and potato salad.

CHILLI POWDER Blended with other spices for use in chilli con carne, tomato chilli sauces and in cheese biscuits.

CINNAMON Add a pinch to lamb roasts and stews. More in apple dishes, with cooked pears and in milk puddings.

CLOVES Use in apple, damson and cherry pies. In tomato soup, veal dishes, pickles, marinades, junket and bread sauce.

CORIANDER SEED For mushroom dishes, spice mixtures and curry powders. Try in milk puddings, fruit fools and with beetroot and sausagemeat.

CUMIN SEED Use in rice and vegetable dishes. Particularly good with aubergines and cabbage. Improves poultry and cheese dishes. Used in curry powder.

CURRY POWDER Commercial mixtures vary in flavour and strength and are mostly over-peppery. Their flavour evaporates quite quickly. Indian cooks mix their own and use different mixtures depending upon the ingredients of the dish. For general purposes (meat) try using 20g/¾oz cardomon, 7g/¼oz cloves, 20g/¾oz cinnamon, 7g/¼oz cumin and a pinch of mace, ground and kept in an airtight jar. This does not make a 'hot' curry but if required, add at most ¼ teaspoon chilli powder to the mixture.

GINGER Use fresh, grated ginger root in oriental type dishes and with conservatively cooked vegetables. Use powdered ginger on melon and in chocolate dishes.

JUNIPER BERRIES Use in marinades for pork and venison. Excellent with duck, pâtés and kidneys.

MACE This is the outer layer of nutmeg and more delicate in flavour. Use in preference to nutmeg where a more subtle flavour is required.

MUSTARD Use dry powder in cheese pastry, salad dressing, rubbed over meat and in sauce for herrings. Use mustard seed for pickling and sprinkled on cooked cabbage. Commercial French and German mustards are more delicate than the English variety, and may be used not only as condiments but also in sauces and salad dressings.

NUTMEG Use a pinch in carrots and spinach. Use in junket and for egg dishes. Good with apple compote.

PAPRIKA Use the real Hungarian sweet variety in goulash, chicken casserole and with strong coarse fish. Excellent combined with soured cream and onions to serve with pork chops. Use as a colourful garnish on egg and cheese dishes.

PEPPERCORNS Use freshly ground black for flavour and aroma in all savoury dishes. Use freshly ground white where a stronger but less aromatic flavour is required. Use sparingly in white sauces.

POPPY SEEDS Use to decorate bread and biscuits. Add to curry dishes. Make a spice butter to dress cooked noodles and vegetables.

SAFFRON For rice, fish and chicken soups, paella. This excellent spice is used extensively in traditional English cookery but is very expensive today.

SALTS Table salt is free-running because of the addition of magnesium carbonate; many people prefer to use rock salt which has no additives, or sea salt which has a good flavour.

SESAME SEED Use in all middle eastern dishes. Also good with pork, sprinkled on bread before baking. Try pan-fried sesame seeds on green salad dressed with sesame oil.

VANILLA Essence is useful for flavouring custards and ice-cream but cannot be compared with the flavour of a vanilla pod. To obtain the best from a pod, make a split in the bean and infuse in milk or cream, add this milk or cream to fruit fools and custards. Wash, dry and use the pod repeatedly, opening the split as necessary.

Note Flavouring essences made by Langdales are recommended for diabetics who need to avoid liqueurs.

Herbs and their Uses

BASIL Use with tomatoes, rich meat and spaghetti sauces. Mixes well with rosemary, sage and summer savory. Try with mushroom dishes, red mullet, chicken and eggs.

BAY LEAF Use in stews, casseroles, sauces, chutney and pickles.

BOUQUET GARNI The basis of this is 1 bay leaf, a sprig of thyme and some parsley stalks tied together and lowered into long cooking stews and casseroles. Or try the herbs you personally prefer, tied in a muslin bag and left in a dish to impart its flavours during cooking.

CHERVIL Add to salad dressings, soups and sauces. With chicken, egg and fish dishes when a more subtle flavour than parsley is required.

CHIVES Use in salads and quiches, added to soured cream with baked potatoes. In cream cheese, omelettes and on scrambled eggs.

CORIANDER Use fresh young leaves in soups and salads.

DILL Use with cucumber salad, green vegetables, stews, poultry and meat. Added to soured cream and served as a sauce for vegetables and fish.

FENNEL Use with fish, veal, sauces and soups – particularly celery soup.

LEMON BALM Use in fish and poultry dishes. May be added to fruit dishes, custards and jellies.

LOVAGE Use in soups – particularly pea and potato. Good with ham.

MARIGOLD Substitute for expensive saffron in rice dishes. May be used in salads, omelettes and cheese dishes.

MARJORAM Used with a heavy hand in Provençal type dishes – long-cooking casseroles, roast meat, game and poultry. Excellent in stuffings and forcemeats. Adds flavour to delicate vegetables such as salsify, carrots and cucumber.

MINT Use with potatoes, carrots and peas. With braised lamb and in mint jelly. Try in fruit dishes, green salads and herb butter.

OREGANO Use as marjoram in Italian tomato dishes.

PARSLEY The all-purpose English garnish. Use in white sauce for fish, herb butter and with new vegetables.

ROSEMARY Use with lamb, chicken and pork. Try with fried potatoes.

SAGE Use in stuffing for pork and poultry – particularly duck. Try a leaf tucked into a veal olive.

SAVORY Use in bean dishes. With eggs, soups and salads.

SWEET CICELY Use in fruit dishes to replace sugar.

TARRAGON Use in Beárnaise, tartare and cream sauces; with chicken, tomatoes, asparagus, artichokes, avocado pears and in salad dressings.

THYME Use in salads, stuffings; with chicken and mashed potato.

QUICK REFERENCE
FOODS AND THEIR EXCHANGE VALUES

The following quantity of foods amounts to 1 exchange:

ALL-BRAN 20g/¾oz
ALMONDS 225g/8oz
APPLES 100g/4oz
APRICOTS, fresh 175g/6oz
   dried, raw 25g/1oz

BANANA, without skin 50g/2oz
   (approx 100g/3¾oz with skin)
BEERS AND STOUTS
   (see page 180)
BEETROOT 100g/4oz
BISCUITS, semi-sweet 15g/½oz
BRAZIL NUTS 225g/8oz
BREAD 20g/¾oz
BRIOCHE ½ average piece

CHERRIES 100g/4oz
CHOCOLATE, drinking
   15g/½oz
   diabetic 100g/4oz
CIDER (see page 181)
COCOA powder 25g/1oz
COCONUT, fresh 275g/10oz
   desiccated neg.
   milk 175ml/6fl oz
CORNFLAKES 15g/½oz
CORN ON THE COB 75g/3oz
CROISSANT ½ average piece
CURRANTS 15g/½oz

FLOUR 15g/½oz
FIGS, fresh 100g/4oz

GOOSEBERRIES, dessert
   100g/4oz
GRAPEFRUIT JUICE,
   unsweetened 6 tablespoons
GRAPES 50g/2oz

HORLICKS powder 15g/½oz

ICE-CREAM, Cornish dairy
   100g/4oz

JAMS, ordinary 15g/½oz
   home-made (see page 21)

LENTILS 25g/1oz

MANGO, fresh 75g/3oz
MARMALADE, ordinary
   15g/½oz
   home-made (see page 22) neg
MELON, cantaloupe 200g/7oz
   watermelon 175g/6oz
MILK 200ml/7fl oz

NECTARINES, fresh whole
   75g/3oz
NOODLES, egg 25g/1oz
NUTS, almonds 225g/8oz
   Brazil 225g/8oz
   hazel 150g/5oz
   peanuts 100g/4oz
   walnuts 200g/7oz

OATCAKES 20g/¾oz
OATMEAL 15g/½oz
ORANGE without peel 100g/4oz
ORANGE JUICE 6 tablespoons
OVALTINE powder 15g/½oz

PASTRY, shortcrust, count flour
    frozen flaky, 212-g/7½-oz
    packet 7½ exchanges
    rough puff, count flour
PEACHES, fresh whole
    100g/4oz
PINEAPPLE 75g/3oz
POTATOES, mashed, boiled,
    roast 50g/2oz
    crisps 20g/¾oz
    sticks 15g/½oz
POURGOURI 20g/¾oz
PRUNES, raw 25g/1oz
PUMPERNICKEL 20g/¾oz

RAISINS 15g/½oz
RASPBERRIES 175g/6oz

RED BEANS, dry 25g/1oz
RICE, uncooked 15g/½oz

SAGO, uncooked 15g/½oz
SAUSAGES, chipolata 75g/3oz
SAUSAGEMEAT 75g/3oz
SEMOLINA, uncooked
    15g/½oz
SPAGHETTI, uncooked
    15g/½oz
SPECIAL K cereal 15g/½oz
STRAWBERRIES 175g/6oz
SULTANAS 15g/½oz

TANGERINES, without peel
    100g/4oz

WAFERS, unsweetened
    10 wafers
WEETABIX 15g/½oz
WHEATGERM 25g/1oz

YOGURT, natural 200ml/7fl oz

Beers and Stouts

Each of the following contains
1 exchange:

600ml/1 pint Konig diabetic lager
600ml/1 pint Carlsberg Pilsner
    lager
300ml/½ pint bottled brown ale
450ml/¾ pint draught bitter ale
600ml/1 pint mild draught ale
300ml/½ pint extra stout
175ml/6fl oz strong ale

Each of the following contains
½ **exchange:**

600ml/1 pint Holstens Diat Pils
    lager
600ml/1 pint Marstons low calorie
    pale ale
600ml/1 pint Whitbread
    English ale

Cider

Each of the following contains
1 exchange:

450ml/¾ pint dry cider
300ml/½ pint sweet cider
150ml/¼ pint vintage cider

Contains no **exchange** *value:*

Bulmers no. 7 cider

FREE OF EXCHANGE VALUE

Meat
Cheese
Fish
Green vegetables
Herbs
Spices
Flavourings
Some fruit – i.e. rhubarb, cooking
    gooseberries, lemons,
    redcurrants, cranberries.
Dry wines, champagne, dry
    sherry
Spirits — i.e. gin, brandy, whisky,
    vodka, white rum

INDEX

The **British Diabetic Association** was founded in 1934 to serve all diabetics. Membership is open to all who are interested in diabetes. Questions regarding diet, employment, insurance, emigration, research, children's holiday camps, the elderly, and other non-medical matters will receive a prompt reply. Donations for research, children, and for general funds are always most gratefully received. The Association publishes *BALANCE*, which is sent to all members free of charge.

Enquiries to:

> **British Diabetic Association**
> 10 Queen Anne Street,
> London W1M 0BD
> Telephone: 01-323 1531

Also in Hamlyn Paperbacks

Jo Foley

THE PICK OF WOMAN'S OWN DIETS

Slimming is something most of us need to do at some time or other. The problem is how to choose from the hundreds of diets available.

This book will help you assess what kind of slimmer you are. Then you can choose from a number of diets specially tailored to suit your appetite and your lifestyle. If you prefer to nibble something every two hours, or if you cannot give up bread, potatoes or alcohol – take heart. With names like the Spice of Life Diet, the 'Help-Yourself' Diet, the Bread and Potato Diet and the Fruit Booster Diet there is something for everyone, be they office worker or housewife, vegetarian or meat lover, gourmet or just plain glutton!

So stop moping about those extra pounds – select the perfect diet for your needs and have fun creating a healthier, slimmer you.

Also in Hamlyn Paperbacks

Attia Hosain
and Sita Pasricha

INDIAN
COOKING

In this practical introduction to Indian cooking
there is a host of authentic recipes – from the
highly spiced, hot Madras curries of the south to
the very different Tikka kababs, Tandoori Murgh
and grilled meats of the north. For real Indian food
is a subtle blend of delicate and exotic flavours
whose 'hotness' can be adjusted to suit individual
tastes. Chapters cover breads, rice, meat, poultry,
fish, eggs, lentils, vegetables, savouries, chutneys,
pickles and other curry accompaniments, as well as
explaining the basic spices and other ingredients
used.

Everyone interested in good food will find **Indian
Cooking** an inspiration and a delight.